Miracles
and How to Work Them

Stories of God working miracles
through one of His children

by
Thomas Rutkoski

Published by Gospa Missions

230 East Main Street
Evans City, PA 16033
724-538-3171
gospa@gospa.org
gospa.org

Amen, I say to you, unless you turn and become like children, you will not enter the kingdom of heaven.

[Mat 18:3]

Contents

Dedication

As a child of God

I dedicate this book

to

The Eternal Father

Acknowledgements

Spiritual Director	Fr. William Kiel
Transcription	Linda Margoni
Editors	Hilary Rojo
	Mary Rutkoski
	Norbert Sieber
Cover graphics	Jason LaFosse
Computer formatting	Donald Gaus
Proofreading	Mary Clare Zedler

My dear friends,

As seeds of faith are planted, we know from Scripture that some fall on rocky soil, have a hard time sprouting and wither away quickly. Some fall among thorn bushes,,and when they sprout, they are soon choked off. Some seeds fall on fertile soil and grow to produce much fruit.

Above is a list of people who donated their time to bring this book to fruition. For the love of God, they gave freely what was given to them freely. Now each of them becomes one of the more blessed workers of the vineyard. These workers are so loving as to help find the tiny plants trying to grow among the rocks and thorns and help them to be transplanted into good soil. They cared so much about you that they labored for free. Please pray for them in grateful thanksgiving.

I, too, will pray for you all the days of my life. Thank you.

In Jesus and Mary,

Thomas Rutkoski

Introduction

Many people, probably including yourself, love to hear of miracles. People are genuinely amazed if they witness someone "work" a miracle. However, can people always believe what they see?

The best way to believe in miracles is not to hear about one or watch someone else perform one. The best way is to work the miracle yourself.

I would like to teach you how to work miracles. This book is meant to be a supernatural "how to" book if you are willing to learn.

It is not child's play. You can work real miracles in the name of the Lord, just as the apostles did, and just as people work real evil with their Ouija boards, crystals, tarot cards and psychic palm readings. Why play with the power of Satan when you can tap into the Power of the Holy Spirit?

Before you begin your journey through this book, please allow me to give you a blessing. I won't tell you what that blessing is just now. See if you can figure it out.

Chapter One

How It Started

Welcome to the Second Book of Thomas. It seems a shame that we hear from only four of the original twelve apostles. A book of Thomas was written, but not accepted by the Church. It recorded the accounts of his walk with Jesus.

How much have we lost by not hearing from Thomas and the other unheard from apostles, especially all the miracles they worked? In John 21:25 it states: *"There are also many other things that Jesus did, but if these were to be described individually, I do not think the whole world would contain the books that would be written."*

How much do *we* miss by not hearing about all of the miracles worked in each one of our lives? I do not surmise that what has happened to me, Thomas Rutkoski, can be compared to what happened to Thomas, the apostle. But possibly you would like to take a close look at how much God has done for me and through me, in the way of miracles. I know full well that God works through ordinary means most of the time. The Lord can be seen working in the rising and setting of the sun. God is alive in a rainbow and a child at play. I pray you will see the Lord working through this book.

Maybe by your reading this book, we can help make up for some lost graces that we all could have received

1

through reading the experiences of Saint Thomas and other seven, "little-heard-from" apostles. We know what an impact the four Gospels we do use (Matthew, Mark, Luke and John) had on Christianity.

Join me in praying that we all can carry on the tradition that Thomas handed down by simply serving the Lord as well as he did. We know that he laid down his life and went on to evangelize the people of India. It is possible to lay your life down today, just as Thomas did back then. I myself am trying to lay down my life and I did not take a paycheck for more than eight years and during that time I actually gained weight. So you see, I am not starving. I have picked up my cross and I am trying to follow the Lord.

I go town to town, telling of the Lord's mercy and the gifts that God gives to His friends. There is nothing to fear. When I go out to speak in churches, I do it for free. I don't even require the people who invite me to pay for the airline tickets. The Lord says what is given freely to you, give freely in return, and I do. The result is that when I go to a town, people feed me and give me a place to stay . If I tear my shirt while there, kind people will offer to buy me a new one. It is called trusting in the Lord.

How do our organization's bills get paid? The night of the presentation a love offering is taken up for Gospa Missions, the nonprofit foundation I began in 1990. Generally, the offering takes care of travel expenses and overhead and there is enough left over to help us do some charitable projects such as building an orphanage in Africa and rebuilding some of the churches that were blown up during the war in Croatia and Bosnia. It's called works. According to Scripture, getting into Heaven requires a combination of faith *and* works.

> *What good is it, my brothers, if someone says he has faith but does not have works? Can that faith save him? If a brother or sister has nothing to wear and has no food for the day, and one of you says to them, "Go in peace, keep warm, and eat well," but you do not give them the necessities of the body, what good is it? So also faith of itself, if it does not have works, is dead. Indeed someone might say, "You have faith and I have works." Demonstrate your faith to me without works, and I will demonstrate my faith to you from my works. You believe that God is one. You do well. Even the demons believe that and tremble.*

> *Do you want proof, you ignoramus, that faith without works is useless? Was not Abraham our father justified by works when he offered his son Isaac upon the altar? You see that faith was active along with his works, and faith was completed by the works. Thus the scripture was fulfilled that says, "Abraham believed God, and it was credited to him as righteousness," and he was called "the friend of God." See how a person is justified by works and not by faith alone.*

> *And in the same way, was not Rahab the harlot also justified by works when she welcomed the messengers and sent them out by a different route? For just as a body without a spirit is dead, so also faith without works is dead.* (James 2:14-26)

And there you have, in a nutshell, my objective in writing this book in the first place . . . getting you and me into heaven.

You are invited by God to work in the vineyard. By reading of my experiences, what I learned and then how I applied that to my life, hopefully you will be encouraged to serve the Lord. I ask Saint Thomas to please pray that I will express perfectly how much God has done for me and through me, so my brothers and sisters will draw closer to Jesus. Please understand that if God would do all of what is in this book for me, most certainly He will do it for you. Just think about giving your life to Him.

If I would dare to compare myself with anyone who followed the Lord before me, I would ask if He has ever done as much for any other person who has walked this planet, as He has done for me. Scripture states, "Saints have longed to see what I have seen and to hear what I have heard." I have seen and heard a great deal, seemingly more than my share. Please pray for me, Saint Thomas, that I do not waste a single effort that our God has invested in me. The phrase, "To whom much has been given, much is expected," crosses my mind frequently.

Wouldn't it be nice if we all experienced miracles in our lives? Do you recall the many miracles listed page after page in the Bible? Then don't think that it is out of the realm of possibility for miracles to happen today. God is the same God today as He was yesterday and as He will be tomorrow. God never changed. *We changed* when we stopped trusting Him. The Father never stopped dispensing grace, mercy, compassion, love and attention to us. He is still here waiting to help at any given moment. The Lord wants to work a miracle in your life today. Consider letting Him do it.

There are parameters within which one should operate to be more susceptible to the miraculous. One of the parameters is to become like a child before God. That requires simple faith and trust. If you are always second-guessing God and wondering why He hasn't answered your prayers, not much in the way of a miracle is coming to you. By questioning Him, you are placing yourself above God. You are figuring that you know the exact moment that the prayer should be answered. What if God knows that ten years down the road is the best time to answer your prayer? Are you willing to wait for His perfect timing?

I am not trying to make you feel bad. No! I want you to feel good. So in these pages which follow, I will relate to you what God did for me after I started surrendering to His will. Please note that for twenty-seven years, I did it "my way" and failed.

Do you remember the song made famous by Frank Sinatra, *My Way*? Sorry, Frank, but Paul Anka, the composer of that song, gave you a bum steer. You and he did it the "wrong way" and the title to your song explains why. A friend of mine, David Parkes, an extremely talented singer and a lay Catholic evangelist from Ireland, puts a twist on Frank's rendition of Anka's song and corrects the error. David beautifully sings, "I Did It **God's Way.**" Life is quite different when you do it "God's Way."

At times, God will work a miracle "out of the blue." He will work a miracle just to let you know He is there. He did that in my life. Unfortunately, most people write them off as mere coincidences. If you play heads-up ball and look for the "Christ-incidences" in your life, then you might find God closer than you first thought.

The reality of encounters with God lies in this basic phrase, "Here I am, Lord. I have come to do Your will." Servants do the will of their master. They do not demand anything. Are you willing to work for God and expect nothing in return? Or do you have this big wish list that God has to fulfill before you believe in Him? God does not need to prove anything to you or me. We need to prove that we love God and thank Him for doing all that He has done for us.

Tom's first book

My first book, *Apostles of the Last Days,* is a miracle unto itself. It is a perfect example of God in action. This man did not have the ability to write a book. I lied to get out of high school. I never read a book in the twenty-seven years that passed between my leaving school and writing that miraculous book. The main reason I couldn't write or read was that I had dyslexia, which was miraculously taken away in 1987.

What I think is truly ironic is that I have never read my own book (start to finish) even though I wrote it. I simply spoke into a tape recorder what was in my heart. Then I called some neighbors and said, "Do you know how to type? Could you come over and type something for me?" One by one, people came to help. To the first person, when she started to transcribe the tape, I said, "Mark this Chapter One." She then started banging away at the keyboard, putting what was on the tape into the computer.

Traveling as an evangelist, I would tell people the stories of my conversion, and as I did, the Lord allowed me to experience more of His wonders. He was creating, through me, more stories for the book. On the way to presentations or on the way home, I would continue to talk into a tape recorder relating what the Lord was placing in my heart. At home again, I would recruit anyone I could find to type what was on the tape recordings. I would say, "Call it Chapter Two." Then chapters three and four were generated in the same manner and finally, there were twelve.

The twelfth chapter really got me excited. I was so excited that I actually sat down to my computer and started pecking away. With one finger at a time, I was trying to hit the right letters to type the last chapter which was the only one I felt I had any part in writing at all. This "hunt and peck" approach took me a long time, but I was impressed with myself upon completion.

During the creation of Chapter Twelve, I dug out an encyclical from Pope Pius XII. The encyclical was of an astounding nature. What it said about the Catholic Church, I truly felt in my heart. Pope Pius XII just hammered home the idea that the Catholic Church is the one true Church. The part which so impressed me was, "Let there be no obstinate wrangling. Salvation lies inside *these* doors, and these doors are open to everyone." I was just eating this encyclical up. I loved it and diligently typed away, including my own comments as I went along. When I was finished, the Lord spoke to my heart. He said, *"Thomas, where did you get that?"* I replied, "Well, I got it from various places, Lord." He asked, *"Could you discard it and type this?"* Out went the entire last chapter and I started over.

Yes, I am one of those "God speaks to me" people. There are no messages for you, just messages for me. God is bent on changing my life and I think He is doing a good job. A person can get in a lot of trouble believing he or she has messages for the world. I would caution you about people like that. Before you fall headlong for visions or messengers, make sure that they are Church-approved or the Magisterium is conducting a serious investigation as to the origin of their messages. False prophets abound everywhere and they outnumber true prophets a thousand to one.

A piece of advice for you. If someone comes to tell you he or she has a message from God or the Blessed Virgin Mary for you, tell him or her to ask God to deal directly with you. God will do that if it was truly a revelation from Him. Don't get me wrong. I know that God has spoken to many people. More than 20,000 times in Scripture, God is documented as being in conversation with someone.

Back to Chapter Twelve. The divine revelation about which I was speaking occurred on the last day that I had to get the book done. It was due at the printer the following Monday to meet the all-important publication date of the day of our June *Retreat at the Farm*. I had to Federal Express it overnight because it was already Saturday. The women who were helping me with the typing thought I was crazy when I tore up the last chapter and threw it out. But this time when Chapter Twelve was finished, I told the people in the room that the new version was what the Lord wanted. The original Chapter Twelve bore not the slightest resemblance to the new Chapter Twelve.

Looking at my watch, I saw that it was about ten minutes to five. "Oh, my goodness," I said. "The Federal Express office closes at five o'clock. I've got to go!" I grabbed the pages and put them in a box and never took the time to read the book in its entirety. It was easy for me to understand that I had nothing to do with this book other than following the Lord's direction. It was obviously God at work.

Racing down to the local Federal Express office, I ran in, huffing and puffing, with only two minutes to spare. I exclaimed to the agent behind the desk, "Look at that. I made it just in the nick of time!" The lady looked at her watch and was astounded. "We were supposed to close an hour ago." A minor miracle! God kept the Federal Express office open an extra hour!

The book *Apostles of the Last Days* is truly, as I said, a miracle. It is filled with exciting stories of how God works in our lives if we just let Him. But that book was just the beginning. It is as the famous radio newsman, Paul Harvey, says, "And now for the rest of the story."

But, with God the story never ends. It is one exciting day after another. If you haven't read my first book, *Apostles of the Last Days*, it might be the best place for you to start. The book is simple to get. Just write to me at 333 Wilderness Trail, Evans City, PA 16033, call Gospa Missions at 724-538-3171 or ask your local bookstore to special order it for you.

Apostles of the Last Days has changed thousands of lives. Many miracles have happened to people while they were reading the book. Your first miracle may be waiting there.

My first miracle

I mention in *Apostles of the Last Days* that the Lord spoke to me. On that day is when I first realized the Lord was working in my life. Jesus speaking to me was my first great miracle. At least the first miracle I noticed or recognized. This is a short scenario of how it happened.

I was sitting on my boat at the Fox Chapel Yacht Club, my preferred watering hole, reading a book about apparitions of the Blessed Virgin Mary. Trying to believe what I was reading was difficult. I was a fallen-away Catholic and was reading that particular book for nonreligious reasons.

The book was in my hands only because I was a photojournalist for a local television station and I was doing research for a possible story. At a moment, as I was reading the third chapter of that book, a voice spoke to me. The voice recounted three places I had been in my life; three places I never planned to go to. I had just stumbled upon them, I thought. In reality, I had even forgotten that I had been to these sites. This voice within addressed me and said, *"Thomas, I took you to Bethlehem, I took you to Lourdes, and I took you to Fatima. Can't you understand that this is real?"*

That one moment changed my life. I ran from the high point of my materialism, my boat at the yacht club, to the closest Catholic church I could find. This visit from the Lord caused me to reenter the Catholic faith after a twenty-seven-year sabbatical. From that moment on, my life has been nonstop, back-to-back miracles.

After this, I visited a place where alleged miracles have happened and received several miracles personally: healings of rheumatoid arthritis, dyslexia and hemorrhoids. Even a wart on my right hand was taken away. And it was all more than I deserved. A previous operation to have that wart removed had failed, but after this miracle day, it never came back. I was not a willing participant in these miracles and came, kicking and screaming, back to the Lord. For the most part I was denying that miracles could happen today. Nevertheless, there I was, living, breathing proof. I walked into the church at this shrine devastated with arthritis and the other ailments, racked with pain, and walked out absolutely healed!

And that's not all. Other miraculous events occurred while I was there. My rosaries changed from the color silver to the color gold. They changed in the palm of my hand in about fifteen seconds. There was also an image of the Blessed Mother that consumed a huge cross on top of a mountain. There she was, but it wasn't yet enough to convince me to give my life to God.

Where is this wonderful place? Places do not matter. The site of a miracle has no significance. It is what you do with your life after a miracle occurs that really counts.

After these miracles, I started to believe some of the teachings of the Blessed Virgin Mary. However, the main theme of her messages I found difficult to absorb. She states, *"I have come to tell the world that God is truth; He exists."* She goes on to explain that if you want to proclaim the existence of God in your life, go to Mass every day, say fifteen decades of the Rosary every day, fast on bread and water on Wednesdays and Fridays, go to Confession once a month, and have conversion of the heart every day. When I first heard this message, I said, "You've got to be kidding. Where could I possibly find that kind of time in my life? Blessed Mother, I don't even believe it is you."

Our Lady patiently walked me through the process. In the course of a visit to one of her apparition sites and all in one day, she got me to say thirty decades of the Rosary and go to Mass twice. She proved me absolutely wrong the very day I declared her message impossible to live. It was as though she was saying, *"Thomas, go home and do just half of that."*

I returned home from my pilgrimage and I did half of what she had me do on that special day. I found the results to be astounding! Mary was teaching me how to love her Son, Jesus.

Generally, you and I only hear about miracles. We love to hear about miracles. I am here to tell you that if you start living the Blessed Mother's messages, you will be astounded with the gifts and grace Mary and Our Lord have in store for you. The message is always the same: daily Mass, fifteen decades of the Rosary each day, fasting on bread and water on Wednesdays and Fridays, Confession once a month and conversion of the heart each day.

Live her message to the fullest extent and you will experience Jesus. You will experience miracles. Not only that, *you will be able to work miracles!* And I don't mean little miracles. I mean great big ones. You will be able to heal the sick and alter the weather - through the Lord, of course. It is great work if you can get it. And you can get it if you try.

The next time a rain storm is in your way and there is a Godly reason to ask that it should end, and if you have enough faith, you command it to stop. When the miracle happens, it will impress even you and it will change your life!

Chapter Two

My Other Mary

Miracles are continuously happening in my life. In the beginning they started out slowly and because of simple requests. After I implemented the message in my life to its fullest extent, I would make a request of God and the request would come to fruition almost immediately. There was one notable exception. It wouldn't happen when I would get in the way.

The first time I realized that I got in the way of God working miracles in my life was when I came back from a pilgrimage and I was burning with the desire to do something for God. I was working at KDKA Television in Pittsburgh, Pennsylvania. My work there consumed most of my time and most of the people I evangelized worked at the television station. But then there was my wife, Mary.

Was my wife getting upset with this God stuff! Browbeating Mary to death with the Lord was easy for me. In wanting her to change as fast as I had changed, it was difficult to understand why she didn't want to hear of all the great things that God was doing in my life. I was away from the Lord for twenty-seven years. My wife Mary had been away for nineteen years. When I would tell her what Jesus was explaining to me, Mary would say, "Well, God isn't speaking to *me*." However, God taught me that badgering Mary was a bad thing to do.

The Lord, in His kindness, would later point out how patient He had been with me and how long He had waited for me, even after He saw no response to His granting many wonderful gifts over many years. I ponder many times how He waited twenty-seven years for my return. Thank God for God!

For too long, all I could do was to relate to those around me what the Lord was doing in my life, yet I couldn't do it at home. But it really feels good at this point in my life to be able to say "we." The reason it feels so good is that the *we* represents me and my wife, Mary. This is the "almost missing" Mary from my first book. Many people ask why my wife wasn't mentioned very much in that book. Many express how they felt, as good as the book was, that something was missing. The reason Mary wasn't mentioned much was because she didn't want to be mentioned in the first book. Using her name in the section that described our wedding was about as far as she was willing to let me go. She was angry about my conversion.

Mary was against my conversion for the first eight years. We fought over God a lot. I can remember Mary saying to me on one occasion, "You love God more than you love me." My answer was, "You've got that right. I do love God more than I love you."

That is how all marriages should be. Both partners need to be in love with God first, or their marriage will never last. If the marriage does last, it will not be a lot of fun.

We can see the fruit of the tree when people get married for lust. Approximately fifty-five percent of all marriages fail today in the United States. If you can find a couple who got married because they love and want to serve God first, each other second, and desire each other sexually third, then you will see a marriage success story.

It is great having Mary with me all of the time now. Well, most of the time it's great. I will never forget how the Lord blessed me with this gift and cross at the same time. Don't get me wrong, our marriage is surviving now better than it has; however, all is not perfect. I see part of my purification lies in our being together all of the time. I pray that I can maintain my zeal for the Lord and that Mary will one day have the same zeal. There is amazing progress being made, thank God, although both of us have to work harder at being examples for others. There is that proverbial plank in our own eye on which we have to keep working.

Mary being with me is a story all by itself. She could write a book for you that would make you laugh. For now you will have to be satisfied with my drastically shortened version of the story of how God put us on the road evangelizing together.

There is no denying that both of our conversions are miracles, and that is the reason they end in a book about miracles. I can see in retrospect how I then, and still do, get in the way of Mary's conversion. Our getting in the way often hampers the miracles that God wants to perform for us and others. If we could simply let God do it His way, we all would be better off.

Many times we all get caught thinking that God needs our input, don't we? Could it be that we think God works too slowly? Well, God knows the precise moment that a miracle will work to its maximum advantage. We, on the other hand, know nothing. If we could understand that we are all nobodies and start all over again from that perspective, life would be better. If the Lord said He was a worm, where do we get off thinking we are something more? And because we think we're what we are not, we encumber God's efforts.

I impeded the work of the Lord in the beginning of Mary's conversion process. I felt she was changing far too slowly. It took God much longer than I wanted Him to. In reality, it wasn't God that worked slowly, it was I causing the stall.

At the beginning of my conversion I would come home and try to share my exciting experiences with my wife. Mary wanted no part of it. Frustration would get the best of me because of not being able to share with her what God was doing in my life. I couldn't share my experiences with Mary, my family, our friends or even the religious around me. When I did, they would push me away. My conversion seemed to be offending everyone. They couldn't take too much of my new zeal.

At home, at least, I expected more of a reception to the miraculous events I was experiencing. I was obviously not a prophet, so to speak, in my own house. God, in His graciousness, allowed me to go into the world and share His mercy with others. "Go and spread the Good News, Thomas. God exists!" Well, this was truly a revelation to me.

After God had paved the way for me, I was invited to speak at many churches around my hometown and then later, outside of Evans City, Pennsylvania. Now I could finally share everything with someone. I tirelessly traveled around the surrounding area giving presentations on my conversion story. If I couldn't have done that, I would have exploded.

You would think that after years of causing friction while trying to evangelize at home, I would give up. Not me. I was going to change everyone whether they wanted to be changed or not. The Lord finally sent me across America and then around the world telling of how He changed my life. God allowed me to continue for many years doing it the wrong way at home. It is great the way God permits wrong to be well established before He pries open one's eye to a situation. I know that this mode of operation is part of His mercy. God then allows us to ponder how stupid we were when we didn't do it the way He wanted it done in the first place.

Most assuredly, and at the perfect moment, the Lord spoke to me again. He used similar words as He did the first time He had spoken to me in August of 1987. If you will recall His profound statement, "Thomas, I took you to Bethlehem, I took you to Lourdes, and I took you to Fatima. Can't you understand that this is real?" His using the word "real," was pertaining to that book on apparitions I was reading. This time He said, **"Thomas! I took you to Bethlehem and I waited. I took you to Lourdes and I waited. I took you to Fatima and I waited. Why are you pushing your wife?"** The light finally went on in my head. All of the time I thought I was evangelizing my wife, Mary, and what I was really doing was making the situation worse.

"I am sorry, Lord," I relented. "I will stop badgering Mary." That was easier said than done, although I did back off some. When I eventually was able to truly reign in my enthusiasm, Mary came closer to Jesus. The Lord was training me to know whom to evangelize full force and how to temper my evangelization of certain other people. It was hard to learn that each person has his or her own way of absorbing God. Different amounts at different times. God is the one who knows the exact moment of each person's conversion. The perfect moment. We generally get in the way of God's perfect moment.

It was frustrating for me to try to bite my lip, but I had to learn to do it God's way. I did then and still do make my share of mistakes. I started working hard at being less of an evangelist at home. In the normal way people in this world operate, this process does not make sense. It would seem to you and me that we need to tell everyone (including our spouses) everything we know about God and all at one time. Then the next day, we have to do it all over again.

I have found out that is the worst thing to do. The Lord explains all this in Scripture when He says, "My ways are not your ways." The only way we can find out that God is always right is to start doing everything His way and be patient enough to see the results.

In backing off my persistent preaching, not only did my wife start coming closer to the Lord, but recognizing this became so exciting to me that I could hardly stand it. Guess who, in his excitement, jumped back in and asked the Lord to speed things up? "Jesus, could you please do something devastating in my wife's life to get her attention?" It was easy to think it was the perfect moment for Him to do more and I wanted it to be done immediately. I was pondering, "If the Lord could give Mary something like cancer or leukemia, she would surely submit to His will."

Most of you must be thinking, "Why in the world would he want his wife to contract some terrible disease?" My thinking is not like that of most people in the world

21

today. At times when I pray for people, they get well. Figuring that if I asked the Lord to make Mary sick, maybe she would start praying for herself and then others would start to pray for her, also. I guess I was throwing some ideas for the acceleration of her conversion up to God, as though He needed my help! To me, the logical conclusion of this situation would be that I could pray over her and the Lord could heal her. Mary then would see that God had restored her to perfect health. The result would be that she would see the goodness of the Lord. Then, realizing that prayer really works, this new understanding of God would catapult her conversion forward tremendously. Again, thank God for God. He chose not to do it my way.

God did hear my prayer, but decided the best thing to do was to take her job away. Mary was the assistant vice-president of marketing for the DeBartolo Corporation, the largest owner, developer and manager of shopping malls in the country and probably the world. She had position, power, authority and she was well-compensated. She traveled to glamorous places and worked with important and famous people.

Mary's job was the most important element in her life. You talk about being devastated. She was shattered when she lost that position. The bad news came out of the blue. Mary was blind-sided by the decision of the DeBartolo Corporation. She always worked long after everyone else had left for the day. She lived and breathed her job and won many awards for excellence in marketing in the shopping center industry. DeBartolo certainly never had a more loyal employee.

It was in the changing of command at the corporation that Mary's problems came. Edward J. DeBartolo, Sr., the founder of the company, had died. Mary's immediate boss also died very suddenly. After company went public, many changes were made. Mary was one of them. God works in mysterious ways.

With nothing for Mary to do other than go looking for another job, I took the opportunity to invite her along on my next speaking tour. I was on my way to Puerto Rico. I knew how much Mary loved to travel and believed if she could only see what it is I do, firsthand, it would help her understand my conversion. This particular time I was right. After an initial rejection, Mary gave in and joined me.

After Puerto Rico I was invited to speak in Alaska, then Chicago and so on. To make a long story short, we have been working together ever since that fateful day early in 1995 as a road evangelization team. Perfect? No, but all is going better now and at God's speed. We go to daily Mass, we say grace at all of our meals and, at times, we say the Rosary and the Divine Mercy Chaplet together. Big improvement!

Mary now works at Gospa Missions headquarters and applies her marketing skills to the Blessed Mother's mission. Her skills are having a great impact on the financial status of Gospa Missions. Previously, for the most part, we didn't know what we were doing in running the financial end of the Mission. People with good hearts came to help, but we were lacking in professionalism and because of that lack, the Mission was under great stress. We needed help badly.

Mary had a positive effect on the Mission, as well as a negative effect. Professionalism between the vendors and Gospa Missions grew. At the same time, those of us who were used to doing things in our innocent, sloppy manner got our feathers ruffled by her. God has His way about Him, doesn't He?

God certainly sent Mary to test us. He possibly wanted to see if we were servants as we claimed. It turned out we were mostly engines with only a few cabooses. Some feathers were not only ruffled, some pulled out of the Mission completely. God's ways hurt at times, but in the long run, we always find out He is right.

Thanks be to God for giving my wife, Mary, to the Mission. I pray that all of the Gospa Missions' staff will be patient with her as she grows spiritually. I also pray that Mary will be patient with all of the Gospa Missions' staff until we get up to speed professionally.

God willing, one day we will all read about Mary's version of her conversion. She has spoken at several events, and at times, has had the audience in stitches.

She can be very funny and, at the same time, be very effective in helping others along the path of conversion.

When I talked to Mary about quitting my job as chief photojournalist for a television station and explained that I was going to start running Gospa Missions for no salary, she became quite upset. She asked how I thought I had the right to make that decision alone. How we were going to make ends meet with our income cut in half? She had a long list of other questions. I don't think I ever answered those questions to her satisfaction. I'm not sure I really knew the answers myself. But did I let that stop me? Not a chance. The Lord said we were to live by faith.

I did have a question for Mary. "If the shoe were on the other foot, if you were quitting your job to do something new, would you expect me to understand?" Not long after that discussion, Mary became more receptive. She really did want me to be happy. After giving her some time to get used to the idea, I resigned my position at the television station.

Again, what at first had appeared to be a huge problem became the source of another miracle, one that really got Mary's attention. We never missed the money. She began to wonder if God was sending her a message in a language she could understand. But when Mary lost her job, the little faith that had built up over those couple of years of operating only on her income, was shaken. When I invited her to work at Gospa Missions for no salary, she said, "How are we going to eat and pay our bills?" My response to that question was then and is still today, "That is God's problem." Mary worked for free, sometimes for ten and twelve hours a day, for five and a half years, and that is another miracle. She now earns a small stipend with the rest of us. Laughingly, she always remarks that she works harder for little or for nothing than she did when she was being well-paid. It is so true.

As we go church to church telling of how God has worked in our lives, people feed us and most always give us a place to stay. It is when we are at home that we have to live off our own resources. The Lord did give us a wonderful financial adviser in Joe Febo and he makes our savings stretch. God's perfect plan for us seems to be: stay on the road evangelizing and you will have few material problems.

To this point, Mary's conversion has been very miraculous. She sees now that a six-figure income can be eliminated and life goes on. However, just wait until Mary tells her story. Many more miracles will happen before this work of God is finished.

Chapter Three

A Prophet

I do not consider myself a prophet, although Scripture says we are all prophets, priests and so on. However, some things that come out of my mouth do come true. As the words fall from my lips, I think to myself, "Why in the world would I say that? How do I know that is true?" Oddly enough, some of my thoughts and statements come true, through the grace of God and for some good reason. The most likely reason they happen is to change me.

As I walk you through these stories, I will talk about me a lot. Please understand that I realize full well that none of this has anything to do with me other than my "yes" to God. It is God who is getting much accomplished, not Thomas Rutkoski.

If God withdrew the grace from me today, I would fall from whence I came. For if it were not for the grace of God, I would already be in Hell. I sincerely understand what a fragile situation I am in.

A few people grumbled about my last book, saying it was too much about me. That is what an autobiography is, a story about the author. Duh!

At one point I had a friend write a very accusing letter to my bishop, charging that I claimed to be a prophet. This man attended some talks I gave and derived his accusation from a statement I had made. Scripture says, *"If you give a cup of water to a prophet you will receive a prophet's reward."* I then added, "If you help Gospa Missions and there is a reward awaiting us, I believe you will share in that reward." And that is true. I hardly claim to be a prophet in that statement. It is a good thing that I tape record my talks because people do get confused, sometimes hear only what they want to hear, misunderstand and then judge. It is our duty to protect each other from false prophets, but you have to be certain that your accusation is true before you harm someone unjustly.

I presented copies of those talks in question to the Diocese of Pittsburgh and the diocese agreed that I said nothing wrong in that series of presentations. This is not to say that in the thousands of presentations I have given that there have not been mistakes. It only goes to show you that it is not good enough to be a human being trying to please God. In fact, you can't even be God without someone judging you and wanting to kill you. We will always have judges and they are only an opportunity to forgive. I have found myself judging others at times also. We, as sinners, tend to do that. I forgive all of my persecutors and pray that everyone whom I have persecuted will forgive me.

Golden glow number one

At times people ask me, when I tell them about a Christ-incidence in my life, if a particular story is actually true. All of the stories I tell are true. If they were not, then I would be back on my journey to Hell.

The following true-life story is from my first book, however, I repeat it here to build a foundation for what follows. You also need to know that this story has upset some people. It is hard for me to understand how someone could read a book where a person pours out his heart and some folks only see something negative. The fact is this story happened exactly as stated and can be verified. Again, it has nothing to do with me; it is God at work. The good part is, I believe, that God sends these little gifts to offset the people that do pour cold water on my or others' conversions or come with their attacks.

There have been times when I have had people say things to me and about me that made me think there was something wrong with them. For the longest time I rejected the things they were saying as ridiculous. There is that judging again. This time, I was doing the judging.

At the second presentation I ever gave, a woman came up to me and remarked, "Mr. Rutkoski, when you were speaking, there was a big golden glow around your head." I replied, "Oh, that's nice," as I smiled at her, but I'm saying in my heart to the Lord, "Lord, could you please keep these kooks away from me?" Instantly I dismissed this woman's observation and wrote it off as her imagination.

Golden glow number two

Not long afterwards, I went to another place to speak. After I finished my presentation, a woman came up to me. She said, "Excuse me, sir. I would like to tell you something. While you were talking, there was a big golden glow around your head." Smiling at her, I said to Jesus, "What is our deal, Lord? Either you keep these kooks away from me or I'll quit doing this. I don't need crazy people hanging around me." Leaving the place shaking my head, I was asking, "Where do they get these imaginative minds ?" Finding either of these women is now almost impossible, so I have no proof that these two scenarios actually happened. But wait.

Golden glow number three

A few days later I spoke somewhere else. After the talk, there was a social in the basement of the church, so I descended the steps with everyone else. Looking around the room, it wasn't hard to see that there was only one open seat. After walking over, I sat in the vacant chair. The lady directly across from me looked straight at me and said, "Okay, I'll tell you." My quick response was, "Excuse me?" She replied, "While you were speaking, there was a big golden glow around your head. I said to the Lord, 'If I tell him he's got a big golden glow around his head, he is going to think I am crazy. So if You want Tom to know this, You bring him over here and put him in this chair.' So there! You have a big golden glow around your head."

In this case, I remember the woman. Her name is Marie Jenkins and we have become friends, so I can back up this story with first person testimony if you need it.

All of this started me wondering what was going on. Why in the world would there be a golden glow around my head and why for just some people? I'm not an angel. I'm not a saint. And I did some horrendous things in my life. Okay, I am trying to clean up my act now, but I had been a very sinful person. There could never be a golden glow around my head.

Hey, mister!

I was speaking in Virginia. After the presentation, a little girl came up to me. I will never forget even her posture let alone her words. She placed one hand on her hip, and because I am very tall, she had to look way up at me. The child said, in her cute little-girl voice, "Hey, mister! Does that bright light shine on your head like that all of the time? And who are those people that stand behind you?" I was taken aback by her statement, but before I could answer her, someone else interrupted and diverted my attention.

When I turned around, the little girl was gone. Her mother is Julie Zackrisson, whom I know, but she was nowhere to be found. When I returned home to Pennsylvania, I called her. When Julie answered the phone, I asked her if I could talk to her daughter Jill. When Jill came to the phone, I told her who I was and apologized to her for not answering her question after my presentation. "Jill, it seems that some people do see things when I go out and speak in the name of Jesus. It is hard for me to say exactly what is happening, but I think that it means that God loves you very much." Jill started to cry. They were big happy tears, of course.

Reflecting on what Jill saw and what she related to me that evening in the church, I thought to myself, "From the mouths of babes..." Again it caused me to wonder what was going on. I asked my spiritual director about it and he said, "When a person is speaking in the Spirit and another is listening in the Spirit, that kind of phenomenon can happen."

On occasion, spanning more than ten years of speaking for the Lord, people will still come up and relate some supernatural phenomenon they see as I speak. Praise the Lord!

Two-thousand roses

As you might imagine, I get a lot of mail because of my first book. It is my prayer that God and all those who have written so many wonderful letters, which I have not answered, will forgive me, but it is impossible to answer them all. There are not enough hours in the day. I still don't type very fast and my handwriting is even worse. A few written replies do come from me, but rather than writing, I try to call. Usually, a call will answer all the questions rather than starting a pen pal relationship. Or the phone gives me the opportunity to thank someone for prayers or kind words or a generous donation. So I am thankful for the people that give me their phone number along with their address.

I am on the road speaking about fifty percent of the year and still have the responsibility of running Gospa Missions and all of its humanitarian projects. In addition, we produce conferences and retreats, publish newsletters, operate a religious goods store, run a religious mail order business and the list goes on. That all makes me a very busy man. In spite of all this, I believe the Lord does entice me to answer some of the letters, so a few people actually receive a written reply.

One day I received a letter from a Sister Antoinette Marie at the Precious Blood Convent in New Hampshire. She wrote, "Dear Mr. Rutkoski, I've read your book *Apostles of the Last Days* and want you to know that it was the first spiritual uplifting I have had in years. You might think this strange coming from a cloistered nun, but I don't know how to pray anymore and am wondering if God hears my prayers."

Those sentences caused me to gasp for breath when I read them. I thought, "How can it be that a cloistered nun would even feel this way?" It was always my impression that these nuns, in their beautiful habits, were the anchors of the ship. How far has Satan infiltrated?

I felt compelled to get in touch with her, so I picked up the phone and called directory assistance for the state of New Hampshire and said, "Do you have a Precious Blood Convent somewhere in the state? Could you look it up?" They found the number and I called.

Upon their answering the phone, I asked the question, "Do you have a Sister Antoinette Marie there?" They said, "Yes, we do." It was like hitting three bars on a slot machine. Jackpot! "Could I speak to her, please?" I would bet that nearly ten minutes went by before a sweet little voice came over the phone. "Yes, can I help you?" I said, "Is this Sister Antoinette Marie?" The reply was affirmative, so I continued.

"Sister, this is Thomas Rutkoski, the author of *Apostles of the Last Days*." Now it was Sister Antoinette's turn to gasp for air. And then I heard, "Oh, Thomas, I was just praying that you would call!" I, of course, was quick to point out, "See that, Sister, it works!" I continued, "Sister Antoinette, this conversation is going to be short today. Tomorrow the sun is going to come out and I want you to go outside and look at the sun. Tomorrow afternoon, I will call you back and you tell me what you saw." She said, "Why in the world would I look at the sun?" "Please Sister, just do this for me," I requested. Then I hung up.

When I called her back the next day I asked, "Sister Antoinette, what did you see?" She responded, "How did you know I would see something?" "Please Sister," I begged, "Just tell me what you saw." She started, "I stared into the sun for fifteen minutes." (We all know that's not possible! This does not mean that you, as a reader, should go out and look at the sun. God was obviously working in a big way in her life.) "Right when I thought I was about to go blind, a big red crucifix went across the sun. What does that mean?" I explained, "That means we are dealing with Jesus Christ and what I am about to lead you through you should do."

Continuing, I said, "Sister, I've sent you two books: the *Pieta* prayer book and Sister Faustina's *Diary on Divine Mercy*. Please read the two books and I'll call you back in a couple of weeks." After hanging up the phone, my mind started to ponder these events. It seems the Lord was not giving her much in the way of an opportunity to respond.

I called Sister Antoinette Marie again about two weeks later and I said, "Sister Antoinette, how are you doing?" She said, in a very excited way, "Oh, Thomas, you know that little blue book you sent me, the *Pieta* prayer book?" She went on to say, "There was a novena in that booklet to Saint Therese. You know, the one who supposedly leaves a rose every once in a while?" I let her know that I was aware of the stories. She explained, "On the ninth day, when I finished that novena, there were *two-thousand roses* delivered to this convent and nobody ordered them!"

Sister related to me what had happened. It seems a florist made a mistake on an order and two-thousand roses were delivered to a local shop. The roses had come by mistake and they were going to be thrown away because it made no sense to return them. The folks at the shop figured that it would be wiser to do something useful with them. They decided to send the roses to the convent before they all died, so the sisters could enjoy them. That is the worldly explanation.

Then Sister went on, "The roses were divided among all of the sisters and I received my share. I thought to myself, 'It wasn't like someone knocked on my door and said, "Here, Sister, these roses are for you." Just as I was thinking that, there was a knock on my door. It was another one of the other sisters saying, 'Sister Antoinette, I got more than my share of roses. Here, these are for you.'" "The exact words she wanted to hear!

I said, "Sister, there you are, tucked away in a convent, cloistered, not seeing the outside world very often and you think God is not paying attention to that. You think that God is not hearing your prayers. You need to know, Sister, that not one prayer has ever gotten by God unheard. But you have to understand that He cannot answer all of our prayers. So often when we pray it is, 'God, I want . . .' 'God, I need . . .' 'God, do this.' 'God, do that.' Real prayer should be more like, 'Here I am, Lord.

I have come to do Your will.' Sister Antoinette, someone prayed very hard for my conversion. Someone made a tremendous sacrifice and through that sacrifice, Christ reached down, almost to the pits of Hell, and retrieved me, a lost sheep. How do we know it wasn't you who paid the price for my conversion?"

Maybe you pray, day in and day out. Do you really think God is not hearing your prayers? He is, and He is sorting out the good prayers from the selfish and putting the good ones to use.

Do we really need to know what God is doing with all of our work and all of our labor? Not wanting to know, not needing to know, and allowing God to be God, is called faith.

If we could just hold out to the end and simply believe that when we pray, it works. We have to get away from the selfish prayers and make them selfless. Don't pray so much for your needs. If you are suffering, offer the suffering to Christ so that your suffering can be united with all suffering. All suffering can be used for the good of the entire flock. There is great treasure being compiled in Heaven through prayer and sacrifice and that treasure is grace. That depository of grace is being used by God every day to save His people and maybe to save people like me and yes, you.

What a better world we would have if we would just accept suffering as sanctifying, pray for others, and make sacrifices for those lost in the world. If we live the Blessed Mother's message of Mass every day, fifteen decades of the Rosary every day, fasting on bread and water on Wednesdays and Fridays, and we contribute the suffering on top of that, it's astounding what our lives in Christ can accomplish. The world would be a far better place if we could get enough people to take this message seriously.

Unfortunately, even some of our priests and bishops are losing faith to the point that they won't teach a message like this, let alone live it. They say it is too encumbering. Do you hear much about daily Mass from the pulpit? Daily Mass is the only place we can get Our Daily Bread, to which the *Our Father* refers. Here is how it is explained in the *Catechism of the Catholic Church* in paragraph 2837:

> "Taken literally (*epi-ousios:* "*super-essential*"), it refers directly to the Bread of Life, the Body of Christ, the "medicine of immortality," without which we have no life within us. Finally in this connection, its heavenly meaning is evident: "this day" is the Day of the Lord, the day of the feast of the kingdom, anticipated in the Eucharist that is already the foretaste of the kingdom to come. For this reason, it is fitting for the Eucharistic liturgy to be celebrated each day.

The Eucharist is our daily bread. The power belonging to this divine food makes it a bond of union.

Its effect is then understood as unity, so that, gathered into His Body and made members of Him, we may become what we receive.

This is also our daily bread: the readings you hear each day in church and the hymns you hear and sing. All these are necessities for our pilgrimage.

The Father in heaven urges us, as children of heaven, to ask for the bread of heaven. (Christ) Himself is the Bread who, sown in the Virgin, raised up in the flesh, kneaded in the Passion, baked in the oven of the tomb, reserved in churches, brought to altars, furnishes the faithful each day with food from heaven."

Satan worked overtime to slow down the teaching of daily Mass because the Bread of Life (our daily bread) will bring about his demise. Through living the Mass, you will help the Blessed Mother accomplish what I perceive to be the biggest project ever assigned to her by Our Lord, which is getting you and me to live the message. Giving birth to Jesus was easy. Getting us to live the message is tough!

I realize that there could be many Protestants and, for that matter, some Catholics, reading this book, who don't realize that Mary is their mother. My intention is not to escalate the ongoing spiritual war with you. I only wish that war were over. Had we all been united and working together, the war may have already been won. I wish that non-Catholics would just stop claiming that we Catholics worship Mary as divine. We do not do that. We cannot do that! She is not divine; she is blessed. But we do love her very much and possibly, because of that, we understand the Scripture that proves her ever virgin.

If the Protestants, in their teaching of the Word of God, would simply understand the reality of John and Mary hearing a directive from Jesus just before His death on the cross, it would clear up some of this division. We would all have another miracle. We would all embrace Mary for what she is, blessed. Jesus said it best. *"When Jesus saw His mother and the disciple there whom He loved, He said to His mother, 'Woman, behold, your son.' Then He said to the disciple, 'Behold, your mother.' And from that hour the disciple took her into his home."* (John 19: 26-27)

A simple understanding of Jewish tradition explains that it is impossible for the Mother of God to have had other children, proving her virginity. It was the custom and the law of the times that when a husband died, the eldest child in the family was to take care of the Mother. When Joseph died, Jesus was then responsible for Mary. Then, as Jesus was dying, this responsibility would have been passed on to the next oldest sibling in the family. But He gave responsibility for His dear mother to a virtual stranger whom He picked up along the way. John then took Mary into his care. There were no other children, no brothers or sisters to whom Jesus could entrust the care of Mary.

The Scripture quote which we Catholics have thrown at us so often is, "Lord, your mother, brothers and sisters are outside." "Who are my mother, my brothers and sisters?" Jesus asked. "Everyone that does the will of the Lord is mother and brother and sister to me." The simple explanation for the use of the term "brothers and sisters" in the Bible is that there was not an Aramaic word for cousins, so the term "brothers and sisters" is used to accommodate this concept. It is similar to my greeting one of my African-American friends with, "Hey, *brother*." Is he my sibling because I used the term "brother" to describe a type of human relationship? Of course not. It is as simple as that.

Many Protestant theologians are starting to understand and to realize that it was Satan who divided us and they are now coming home. People like Scott Hahn and Gerry Matatics. There is even an organization called Coming Home International which was founded to support the increasing number of Protestant ministers who are finding their way back into the Church Christ founded. Thank God!

Satan convinced Martin Luther that the pillar and foundation of the Church was by Word alone. Protestants teach that if something isn't in the Bible, it is not to be believed. What is truly ironic is you won't find that premise anywhere in the Bible! In reality, it is the Word and Tradition that Scripture teaches us to use as the basis for our religion. The Church is the foundation. The Church has those in authority appointed to direct her, but she also has those who defy that authority. Always has; always will.

"I have written something to the church, but Diot'rephes, who likes to put himself first, does not acknowledge my authority. So if I come, I will bring up what he is doing, prating against me with evil words. And not content with that, he refuses himself to welcome the brethren, and also stops those who want to welcome them and puts them out of the church. Beloved, do not imitate evil but imitate good. He who does good is of God; he who does evil has not seen God." (3 John 1: 9 - 11)

What a mess we've gotten ourselves into. God said, "Do not divide the wheat from the weeds; the angels in the end times will do that." Again, we didn't listen to God, did we? We are so divided now that we have twenty-seven-thousand different denominations of Christianity. Which one is right? Don't we need a miracle or two to fix all of this bickering and lack of loving one another?

The Blessed Mother is never offensive to someone who understands the truth. She is part of the perfect family: God is our Father, Jesus is our friend and brother, and Mary is our mother. Is anyone happy about losing his or her mother? Of course not, because everyone wants a complete family. Everyone wants a mother. Mary is our heavenly mother. She is the Mother of all people given to us when Jesus, from the cross, told John, *"This is your Mother."*

So, my protesting friends, don't be so obsessed with how many pictures of George Washington you are carrying in your wallet and start carrying a picture of your Mother. And stop offending Jesus by telling the world that His mother is only a woman. She is the only woman divinely chosen to carry God in her womb for nine months. She is a living tabernacle. If there were ever a human being you should *not* criticize or belittle, it is Mary, the mother of Jesus. Wow! I wouldn't want to have to pay that debt to the Lord.

Remember the words of Elizabeth, Mary's cousin, whom she visited shortly after she conceived Jesus through the Holy Spirit, *"But who am I that the mother of my Lord should come to me?"* (Luke 1:43)

Embrace Mary as your mother and you will experience miracles in your life. Or do you believe you can experience miracles in your life even while brushing her aside?

Scripture says, *"Many will say to me on that day, 'Lord, Lord, did we not prophesy in your name? Did we not drive out demons in your name? Did we not do mighty deeds in your name?' Then I will declare to them solemnly, 'I never knew you. Depart from me, you evildoers.'"* (Mat 7:22 - 23)

Who are these people to whom Jesus is talking?

I could write a whole book on the false impressions that the people have regarding the Catholic Church. Indeed, good books on this subject have been written, many by former Protestants who now understand the errors in their once steadfast beliefs. It is remarkable how hard the Church has tried to reach out to all those separated from her. Most of the statues in our churches have been stored in closets, attics or basements, sold for pennies or destroyed completely. In many churches (now liturgically referred to as "worship sites" or "worship spaces") there is no evidence of a kneeler and most of the beautiful paintings and murals have "disappeared" from their walls. Some of our new churches are built without stained glass. We installed immersion pools to accommodate adult baptisms to make Protestants more comfortable. Protestant scholars were allowed to help write the Catholic Bible to make it their Bible, too, and still so few come home. All of this, plus turning our cheek, "seventy times seven" each day and trying harder still, is our attempt to welcome back all the separated.

To all our Protestant brothers and sisters, "Please, come home." Jesus is waiting. We love you and He loves you, but He wants us all in one flock. That is the miracle that Jesus wants today. Will you please try to work the miracle of unification for Him? We started with one Christian denomination and now there are, as I said, twenty-seven-thousand Christian denominations. We have to get back to one.

Do you want me to be a prophet? Then let me prophesy this: when we all unite in the one true faith, we will be only a breath away from Heaven.

Down syndrome baby

Joan and Jim Workman from Richland, Washington, are fairly new friends of Mary's and mine. We lost most of our old friends when we turned our lives over to God. The kind of friends that the Lord has given us now are truly gifts. The Workmans, along with Don and Bonnie Klippstein (also from Washington), have set up many speaking engagements across their state to allow me the opportunity to evangelize. As a team, we work to rebuild the Catholic Church in America. In the state of Washington, there is much to be done. They tell me that this is the most "unchurched" state in our country. I guess that makes Washington mission territory. Not only is it a place where you can introduce folks to the Universal Church, but the sparsity of Catholic churches and orthodox clergy seem to be similar to the conditions under which Jesus trained his twelve apostles. It is all very exciting and a very good place to work a few miracles.

Jesus worked miracles so the twelve would learn how to perform them. Through the power of the Holy Spirit and after they understood the process, these twelve men went out into the world and worked miracles of their own. All of this was done to gain the attention of people and to unveil the truth. They understood, and tried to make the people understand, that it is the truth that would set them free, not the miracles. However, never forget that the miracles were needed to open the door for the truth.

Someone can throw this Scripture at you, *"It is an evil age that seeks signs and wonders."* However, you cannot pick one sentence from Scripture and try to determine what it, standing alone, means. This is probably the key to everything and is the reason why many people fall into traps. The Bible is very complex, so don't let some fundamentalist talk you into believing that we don't need miracles. Miracles are now, and always have been, a part of God's complex plan.

On the other hand, you have to be very careful about people who come only to impress you with signs and wonders. *"For false Christs and false prophets will arise and show great signs and wonders, so as to lead astray, if possible, even the elect."* (Mat 24:24) A person truly working for the Lord is humble, gives all of the credit to Jesus and consumes His Body and Blood. You have to check out the miracle workers.

It seems that it does bother the Lord somewhat to resort to working miracles. It is fairly certain that He would prefer that we believe in Him without the visual aids, but He must understand that we humans need the help. *"Jesus therefore said to him, 'Unless you see signs and wonders you will not believe.' The official said to him, 'Sir, come down before my child dies.' Jesus said,*

'Go, your son will live.'" (John 4: 48-51) The man believed the word that Jesus spoke and went his way. As he was headed home, his servants met him and reported that his son was going to live.

There are literally dozens of cases like this where the Lord worked wonders to advance the faith of the flock. And then, how many were not recorded? So if the Lord tells us that we, if we believe, will work greater wonders than He, let's get started!

There are so many memorable moments from my Washington trips that I could share with you, yet one truly stands out. I was speaking at Saint Patrick Church in Pasco, Washington. In the course of the evening, Jim Workman came up to me and said, "There is a woman outside wanting to talk to you."

"Tell her to come inside," I said. He explained to me that she was a Protestant and she wouldn't come into a Catholic Church. I went outside and found her standing there with a child in her arms. "Yes, ma'am, can I help you?" I asked.

"They say you pray for people and they are healed. Do you pray for Protestant people as well?" she questioned.

"Some people do receive a physical healing from the Lord when I pray for them, and yes, I do pray for Protestant people. We are all God's children. What is the problem," I asked?

"It's my baby," she said as she uncovered the child. With the child exposed, I could see that it was, in my layman's estimation, a Down syndrome child or some other birth defect. She gave me no explanation of what she knew to be wrong with the baby.

When I say the child had a birth defect, I only use that term because that is what most people understand to be the case. In reality, these so-called abnormalities are not birth defects at all. These children were given to their specific parents as a gift from God.

The first thing most people say when I relate this theory to them is, "Do you actually think God would purposely do this to us?" But I say to them that you can never realize the gift until you thank God for it and live your life knowing that God gives gifts like Down syndrome children. I know one boy who is a Down syndrome child. His name is David. His parents treated him as if he was a gift from God. Guess what? He is. David is a wonderful young man now. I would be honored to have a son like him. So then, why pray for someone who is Down syndrome? Only to witness the manifest glory of God and to see lives change when people witness His great works. With God, all things are possible.

Laying my hand on the baby's head I said, "I bless you with the blessing of the Blessed Mother and may the power of the Holy Spirit come upon you." It was the same blessing I use every time I pray over someone. The only other words we exchanged, outside of my inviting her to become Catholic, were, "Thank you." I never found out their names. She left and I returned inside the church to finish my work. Fulfilling all of my commitments at the schools and churches that were set up for me in Jim Workman territory, I then returned home.

The following year I returned to the same area. Washington had become an annual tour for me through the hard work of the Workmans and the Klippsteins.

At one of the churches, after my presentation, we were invited to join everyone in the church social hall for a snack. While I walked through the crowd, Jim Workman again came up to me and said, "There is a woman here who would like to talk to you." Walking over, I then introduced myself to her. She said, "Don't you remember me?" I looked at her and tried to recall if I had met her somewhere, but to no avail. My memory is terrible when it comes to people's names and faces. Normally I turn my bad memory into a joke and tell people that it is from eating food cooked in Teflon pots for so long. Now everything just slides right off my brain. My wife, Mary, on the other hand, remembers everyone. I think that is why God has her on the road with me now. We are a good team. I talk about God to people and she reminds me who they are.

I said to this woman, in a sad way, because it breaks my heart not to remember people, "No, I can't place you." She then asked, "Do you remember my baby?" "No, I can't say that I do. Have we met before?" "I am the

Protestant woman who asked you to come out of your Catholic church and pray for my baby last year."

The light went on. "Oh, I remember you now." I did remember the incident, but I couldn't remember what was wrong with the child. She showed me her baby and pronounced, "Look!" The woman obviously expected me to see some difference, maybe some miraculous difference. I didn't know what to say because I didn't know what the miracle was and I was too embarrassed to ask. "Well, we just wanted to say thank you," she replied. "Thank God if He gave you a gift," I said. That is always my standard reply. The healing has nothing to do with me, so what else can I say, but "thank God"?

Not really knowing exactly what the difference was, nevertheless realizing that she knew her baby received some kind of miracle, I inquired if she were going to become Catholic. The answer was yes; that she was in the process. I replied, "Well, may God bless you. Thanks for sharing your experience with me," and I walked away. To me the real miracle was her becoming Catholic.

Jim Workman followed along with me and said in a very surprised manner, "You really don't remember? That child was Down syndrome or something like that. I remember when you prayed over the baby. I saw how the child looked."

What can any of us say but "Thank God"? Did we not believe God when He said to ask anything of Him, in the name of Jesus, and it would be granted? Aren't we all doubting Thomases most of the time? Even when I know these things are possible and they happen to me or through me, each situation is hard to believe. No matter how many times it happens, it causes me to think, "Is this really true? When will I stop doubting?"

At my presentations, I give examples of exactly how many people don't believe that Jesus is truly present in the Eucharist. Daily Mass attendance is very minuscule in most places of the world. Even on Sunday, under threat of what used to be called mortal sin (the kind that can send you to Hell for all eternity) only twenty-seven percent of Catholics, on average, come to Mass. How can it be that people can proclaim a belief that Jesus Christ is alive in every tabernacle in the world and know that they can actually go and visit Him any time they want and then not show up very often? To know that you can touch God seven days a week, two times a day, and yet choose not to do so, speaks volumes about what you believe and what is truly important in your life. To say we believe and then act in a lackluster way is foolish. Do not our actions speak far louder than our words? We are placing far too many things in our lives before God and it falls back to our disbelief in the Real Presence.

I'll tell you the truth. I know how I can get people into church. It would be easy for me to fill every church to capacity and beyond. I know the god of my brothers and sisters of this world. It is the god of money!

Attendance at one of my presentations, usually held in a Catholic church, is one to three hundred people. We feel dwarfed in a church that seats fifteen hundred. What is truly a shame is that many parishes have more than two thousand registered parishioners, and only a handful come. To those who are present, I say, "If I put a million dollars on the altar and tell you to come up and take some, everybody in the church would come up and take some. Tonight that would not be a problem, for you are already here and you have received Jesus today. (Before all of my presentations I ask to have the Rosary prayed and Mass celebrated.) The real problems will be overcome when I invite you all back tomorrow and tell you I will have more money here. The next day everyone will alter their entire day to attend. Not for Jesus, but to get some more of the cash."

Not only will people alter their day, they will become evangelists for their "money god." They will bring their friends and neighbors. Whatever was going to be important for them that next day, they are not going to do. They are going to come to church for the money. In fact, there will be a traffic jam that second night. Not only will people come the second night, but to every talk where I am giving a million dollars away. I would become the most famous evangelist in the world, because money is the god of most people.

What does that say about Catholics? We have to get a lot of things changed in our lives if we are going to proclaim our belief that Jesus Christ is alive, Body, Blood,

Soul and Divinity, in the one, holy, catholic, and apostolic Church. We've got to stand behind our proclamation with action. When God sees us acting as though we believe, He will send the grace to enable us to work miracles. Will we make mistakes? Yes! Should that stop us from trying? No!

Little girls pray

I was speaking at a church in the diocese of Scranton, Pennsylvania. After I had finished giving my presentation, I was preparing to give the blessing of the Blessed Mother, as I usually do. But first I said to the audience, "I have the strangest feeling that you think that this blessing has something to do with me. If a person is giving his life to God and then God works through him, that doesn't mean that there is something special about the individual. The real process of how all of us should be operating, according to the Gospels, has simply begun in that one person.

If you are employed to make, say, a car part and you make it every day, that doesn't make you special; it makes you a car part maker. You are just doing what you were hired to do. So when you finally start doing things the way God instructed from the beginning, it doesn't make you special. It is only you responding to your Creator as you should have been doing all of your life. Thanks be to God for not holding our late starts against us.

To continue: At times I get the feeling people look at me as though I am something different or more blessed than they are. I am not. So I said to this group, "To show you that God will work through anyone, I would like to call some of you forward to do the blessing instead of me." Scanning the room looking for some likely candidates, I saw several young girls sitting in the middle pews. They were all around the age of twelve and sitting together.

Calling them forward, I asked if they would help me. Their answer was yes, so I then laid my hand on each one of the girl's heads and gave them the blessing of the Blessed Mother. Continuing, I invited the audience to come forward and receive the blessing from the children. To the amazement of the audience, there was no difference between receiving the blessing from me or from the children. People all through the church were being slain in the Spirit. They were receiving physical and spiritual healings at the same rate as if I were doing the blessing myself.

A great big smile appeared on my face. I was so happy. It was actually more fun getting other people to work miracles than working them myself. Especially children! Why? Because it is all part of the process that God has laid down in Scripture that so few of us ever take seriously. He tells us to get the plank out of our own eye then go and help our brothers and sisters get the speck out of theirs. I walked back and forth helping the girls as they needed it. I helped them with the words of the blessing and explained what was happening when someone would go out in the Spirit. After the blessing was over, the girls and I thanked God together for using us in such a fashion.

At the end of the evening I walked to the back of the church and found a woman crying. I asked her why. The woman explained that one of the children called forth to do the blessing was her daughter and the rest of the children were in her daughter's prayer group. She said, "My daughter somehow received a copy of your book and read it. The other girls you picked and my daughter then started to do what you asked for in the book. They started a prayer group and I found them one day giving each other that blessing. I got very angry with them and told them they were making a mockery of God and insisted that they stop and never play games like that again."

"How could it be," the mother said to me, "that you would come to this parish and call those very girls forward and have them do the blessing?" My explanation was that we are all called to give blessings. God Himself calls us to bless Him. Just a few examples:

> *I bless the Lord who counsels me.* (Psalms 16:7)
> *I will bless the Lord at all times.* (Psalms 34:2)
> *In your choirs, bless God, bless the Lord.*
>   (Psalms 68:27)
> *Sing to the Lord, bless His name.* (Psalms 96:2)
> *I bless the Lord, my soul, all my being, bless His holy name!* (Psalms 103:1)

The list goes on and on. If God calls us to bless Him, how much can we bless each other? Our Lord orchestrated this presentation, which included the girls doing the blessing, to deal with this mother's problem. It shows how much God is interested in each one of us.

Don't stop people from being imitators of God, but encourage them to walk in the path of the Lord. These girls were already walking the path of the Lord and that doesn't make Satan happy. It really ticks Satan off when you get children to believe in God.

Dallas blessing

A similar scenario happened in Carrollton, Texas, near Dallas. After my talk, I called some children forward to give the blessing once again. I gave them some basic instructions, I prayed over them and we started. The same results occurred. Many people received gifts from the Lord through the children. As they prayed over people, I would go child to child coaching and explaining that God was working through them. The children were told that this didn't make them more important, but allowed them to experience the power of God.

Everyone could see that the kids were very moved by the experience. Some of the children even started to cry. You have to admit, to have adults come to children and have their little hands placed on adult heads and see the adults fall over in the Spirit, has to be a life-altering experience for everyone concerned.

Several of the children came to me and related that they never knew that God could be so real. I took them all in front of the tabernacle and had them all kneel down. I explained how we were working for the Lord and what it meant to pray over the people. It was also explained to them that anytime you have the privilege of working in the name of the Lord you should always take time to thank Him. What better place than face to face in front of the Tabernacle? I continued telling them that Jesus was truly present and we could talk to Him and explain all of our problems to Him.

God wants us to talk to Him and praise Him. It won't be a one- way conversation, because God will talk back. Remember those twenty-thousand times in the Bible that a conversation takes place with the Lord. I wanted them to know that God was not boring, that He could be our best friend if we just let Him. From me came the explanation that working for God was the best job in the whole world.

One young girl, about fifteen years old, came over to me after we had finished. She said, "I never considered being a nun in my whole life before tonight, but now I am going to think more about that." Another miracle! Anytime you can change the course of a child's life and get her to consider a religious vocation, God was at work and that is miraculous. For me, the seal of confirmation that God really was at work came when I experienced an attack by Satan.

One of the parishioners later wrote me a letter. She told me she was on the evangelizing committee and parish council at the church where I spoke. She then related how upset she was over the children being subjected to such nonsense and that I should be ashamed of myself for involving them in such things. The letter was long and the second greatest chastisement I had ever received concerning my evangelizing to that date.

The condition of that parish, the way the church looked physically, their track record of vocations and the attendance at Mass there, spoke loudly of the effectiveness of their form of evangelization and theology. It was a liberal parish and it had all but killed the faith of those concerned.

Many of the people that want to destroy our tradition think that no one notices that we are down to twenty-seven percent attendance at Sunday Mass. They can't see that sitting in a pew one hour a week is not faith. It is apathy. Worse than simply being apathetic, they impede others who want to show the world that God exists. I threw that letter in the trash. Letters like that only drive me all the more to help children understand how wonderful our God is. If you want to know how well we have done with our children in our spiritual teaching of them, ask how many of them want to be priests and nuns. That is something I ask at all of the Catholic schools before I speak to the children. The answer is almost always zero. At the end of my presentations I ask again and a percentage of the children are then interested. But without the proper foundation, how long can that little seed I planted last?

Someone is actually talking our children out of being priests and nuns. Their teachers tell them in school to be doctors and lawyers and then at home they hear the same. How in the world will we replace the diminishing number of our priests and nuns if no one is going to tell the kids that working for God is a wonderful thing to do? How can they survive in this deteriorating world if God isn't presented to them in an exciting way?

After a talk in one Catholic school (and I do speak in non-Catholic schools,) I had several little children come up and start hugging me. One child said, "Will you remember me the rest of your life?" Not only will I remember her, but now a lot of people will remember her.

One boy asked a very difficult question. These kids have many difficult questions, but God always comes through for me. This young man asked, "How can God be everywhere at one time? I cracked up and said, "Why don't you ask me a tough question?" The Holy Spirit was on the ball that day; in fact, that is what came to mind - a ball. The explanation went like this: "Think of a basketball. It has no beginning and no end. It's just round. That is the way God is also. He has no beginning and no end and He is around, always around."

The children want to know about God, but they have people teaching them about God who themselves do not

Thomas Rutkoski

believe. How can instructors bring excitement to a subject in which they have little faith or even interest? We need some miracles in this area also! When I speak at the schools, I tell the children about the miracles in my life and it changes their lives. They just love to hear about miracles.

Chapter Four

No Cowards in Heaven

Give him your cross

I was speaking for the first time in Salt Lake City, Utah. Afterwards, a woman invited me to come to her home to pray for her son. That in itself was not an unusual request. Many times people will ask me to come and pray for their loved ones who could not make it to the talk. This particular time my talk ended around 11:00 p.m. I was only scheduled to be in Salt Lake City for that one night and fly out in the morning. If I were to pray for this woman's son, it would have to be that evening.

I asked her how far she lived from the church. She replied that it was about an hour away. As I swallowed hard, thinking to myself . . . about three hours round trip and that would not get me back to my hotel until 2:00 a.m. That would mean that I will only get a few hours sleep. Then I caught myself and I thought of how God doesn't waste my time or His own by having someone ask me to do something that He hadn't planned. Not my will, but Your will be done, Lord.

David Trujillo, the man who set up that evening's speaking engagement, and several of his friends, accompanied me and we went with the lady. When we arrived at her home, we found out that her son was a paraplegic. We were introduced to the young man, who was still up at that late hour, and were instantly impressed with how well he negotiated the wheelchair where he spent all of his days. He was a robust, well-groomed and muscular young man. It seemed a shame that such a handsome and otherwise healthy boy should have to sit in a wheelchair all of his life.

Many times I am moved to tears when I meet the people for whom the Lord wants me to pray. A great feeling of compassion comes over me as I plead their cases before God.

I began pleading this boy's case before the Lord. My hand moved to his head and I proceeded to give him the blessing. "I bless you with the blessing of the Blessed Mother and may the power of the Holy Spirit come upon you." As I was praying, the Lord said to me, *"Give him your cross."*

I did not understand what the Lord meant. If I had indeed picked up my cross and followed Jesus, then how could I give that cross to this boy? Then I clutched the cross that I wore around my neck and thought, "You don't mean for me to give him this cross?" I heard in my head, *"Yes, the cross around your neck."* I instantly answered, "Oh Jesus, you couldn't possibly want me to give up this cross."

You, the reader, have to understand how much this cross meant to me. It was given to me by a very kind friend. It contained relics of seven saints and a relic of the true cross. I wore this cross at all of my presentations. It was becoming like my trade mark and very dear to me.

"How badly do you want this boy healed?" Jesus asked? I responded, "Very badly, Lord." "Then give him the cross."

Reluctantly, I took the cross from around my neck and said to the boy, "Here, Jesus wants you to have this." I explained the significance of the cross and the importance of it in my life. I let him know that this was not an easy thing for me to do. The cross had been with me throughout all of my evangelizing. I explained to the boy that when I would ask God for a miracle in someone's life, I would hold onto that cross and ask the intercession of all the saints who were represented in the cross.

Separating myself from the cross was difficult, so I paused for a moment. Then someone else arrived on the scene. Guess who? Reaching into my back pocket, I removed my wallet. I took out one of my business cards and handed it to the boy. I said, "Here, take this card. It has my address on it. As soon as you are walking, please send my cross back!"

I didn't think so at that moment, but I later realized what a stupid thing that was to say. Why would I question what God is asking me to do? Why would any of us question Him?

The boy was not cured that night. Jesus may have wanted to grant him a physical cure immediately, but perhaps my being selfish interfered. I do not know this for a fact, but a few days after I left Salt Lake City, I believe the Lord taught me a lesson.

After my conversion, there were only two possessions that I truly loved. One was the above-mentioned cross and the second was a sterling silver rosary I brought back from Czestochowa, Poland. Most all of the junk I had collected in my life I'd gotten rid of. These two sacramentals were the whole of my cherished earthly goods.

I was now back home in Pennsylvania and working late at Gospa Missions one day. Suddenly I realized that there was something I needed from the Giant Eagle grocery store in Cranberry Township for my next trip. I jumped into my car and raced off. Most times when I am in the car, I pray. On the way to the store I started to pray the Rosary. As I approached the shopping area, I laid my rosary on my lap. I then pulled into a parking place. After parking, I forgot about the rosary on my lap and jumped out of the car. I ran into the store as fast as I could, for it was raining hard.

When I returned to the car, I got in, started the car, and drove off. Shortly up the road I remembered to continue praying the Rosary. Reaching into my right front pocket where I always kept my rosary turned up nothing. The rosary was not there. Nervously searching, I started to think of when I had last used it. Then I recalled placing it on my lap before I got out of the car at the market. In a panic I turned around and went back to where the car was parked to search for it. It had to be right where I had gotten out. It was still raining hard, but that did not matter nearly as much now as it had earlier. I searched the whole area, but it was nowhere to be found. I went into the store and asked if anyone had turned in a rosary. The response was negative. I reached into my back pocket and pulled out my wallet. I took out one of my business cards and gave it to the store manager so he could call me in case it turned up.

I returned to my vehicle and started to drive back to Gospa Missions. It then dawned on me, the way I gave the business card to the manager. This could have been the Lord teaching me a lesson about the folly of becoming attached to material possessions. I was reluctant to give up my cross and gave the boy my card so I could get my cross back after the Lord worked His miracle. I was devastated to lose my rosary. I left my card at the grocery store in an attempt to get the rosary back. I thought, "This is too similar not to be a Christ-incidence."

I learned from this scenario and many others that attachment to material possessions is not a good thing, even if they are religious in nature.

The following year I returned to Salt Lake City where Gospa Missions sponsored an all-day *Retreat in the Mountains*. At the end of the day, I said to my friends, "I want to pay a surprise visit to the paraplegic boy." They remembered where he lived, so off we went. We were greeted at the door by the boy's mother and excitedly she went to get the young man. When he came from his room, I could see that there had been no miracle in his life at that point. I was somewhat disappointed by that.

I noticed that he was not wearing the cross that I had given him. I shook his hand and asked where the cross was. He responded, "It is in my drawer in my bedroom." "How do you expect a miracle to happen if you won't even wear the cross that Jesus gave you?" I asked. The boy said, "I don't know if I want a miracle."

How in the world can someone sit in a wheel chair, paralyzed from the waist down, and not have a strong desire to walk again? That puzzled me for a moment.

I said, "Regardless of whether you want to walk again or not, you can do a tremendous job for the Lord if you wore the cross, if only for the conversations it could cause. If you want to stay in your wheelchair, stay there with a smile on your face and show people that you love Jesus Christ. Show the world that because of Him, you can deal with your situation. You could be a great evangelization tool and help many people who are in the same state in life."

I was starting to understand that he was frightened of being able to walk again. It would mean that he would have to accept a tremendous amount of responsibility. There would be no one to wait on him, fulfilling his every need. He would have to find a job, become a contributing member of society. There would be no more hiding behind a wheelchair and a disability. When looking at the world from a point of security, I guess he must have felt more comfortable not having to deal with the world and all of its problems. I am sure that is not true for all disabled people, but seemed to be the case with this boy.

I told him to get the cross out of the drawer. He rolled over and retrieved the cross. I put it around his neck and told the boy to wear it always. I insisted, "Stop being a coward and accept the gift that God wants to give you. Then you could go out and tell the world about what God did for you." I gave him, as well as the rest of his family, the blessing of the Blessed Mother, just as I did on my first visit, and we left.

Most certainly this is not the end of this story. It is an example of how God tries to work in our midst. Sometimes we are the stumbling blocks that get in the way of the Lord. Both myself and this young man made mistakes and have probably caused this miracle to not happen. I pray to God for the grace for both of us to learn from this experience and to become better and more responsive tools for the Lord in the future.

Ralph and Lorraine

If you had read *Apostles of the Last Days,* you would know that Lorraine Mutschler, one of Gospa Missions' first volunteers, spent many months helping me work on that book. She became a very dear friend. It was not an easy task for Lorraine to come and help me. Lorraine had to drive forty miles in each direction, every day, to volunteer her services.

Eventually a tremendous test came into her life. Her husband, Ralph, had just retired from Bell Telephone. Shortly after his retirement, he started to experience great pain. He refused to go to the doctor until after their upcoming family reunion and wedding of his youngest daughter.

On July 13, 1993, Ralph finally went to the doctor. Many tests were performed and, from the tests, the doctors decided to do exploratory surgery. On Ralph's 61st birthday, July 26, 1993, he was taken into surgery. Bad news came quickly. The surgery was to take four hours, but the doctor returned in only 40 minutes. Dr. Fingeret, the surgeon, had tears in his eyes as he told Lorraine that he had found that Ralph had adenocarcinoma, a terrible kind of malignant tumor.

They had not done the surgery because Ralph's abdomen had been full of these large tumors and there was nothing they could do. The doctor then explained that Ralph had about three months to live, that his own father had died of the same disease, and that it was going to be a very painful and difficult death.

With this bad news, Lorraine had to stop coming to work at Gospa Missions in order to take care of her husband. She would fill me in on his status over the telephone. Soon Ralph started to deteriorate very rapidly and Lorraine asked if I would come and pray for him. Obviously, I agreed. I procured help from my friend, Toby Gaines, and we went to the hospital to visit and pray for Ralph.

Lorraine was at the hospital when we arrived. She took us to Ralph's bedside. Toby and I walked over to Ralph and laid our hands on his head and prayed for him. It was obvious that he was in very much pain.

By this time in my life, many miracles had happened to people for whom I had prayed. Lorraine, being as close to me as she was, knew this. It seemed to me that I could see in her eyes the great hope she had for a miracle. My not wanting her to lose confidence in what God was doing in my life caused me to say something I should not have said. I told Lorraine that I believed that God was going to take Ralph home to heaven. He really looked like he wasn't going to survive.

I didn't say that I thought the Lord was taking Ralph home because I had some kind of inside information. I was setting myself up for spiritual protection. I was afraid of falling into the realm of being a false prophet.

It is not easy to proclaim that a miracle is about to happen. If I didn't have the guts to do that, what I could have said to Lorraine was, "It's in the Lord's hands now." That is always an easy copout or safer yet, I could have said nothing at all. That particular time I was a coward and not a very faithful servant of the Lord.

> *Speak not to a woman about her rival,*
> *nor to a coward about war,*
> *to a merchant about business,*
> *to a buyer about value,*
> *to a miser about generosity,*
> *to a cruel man about mercy,*
> *to a lazy man about work,*
> *to a seasonal laborer about the harvest,*
> *to an idle slave about a great task,*
> *pay no attention to any advice they give.*
> *Instead, associate with a religious man,*
> *who you are sure keeps the commandments,*
> *Who is like-minded with yourself*
> *and will feel for you if you fall.*
> *Then, too, heed your own heart's counsel,*
> *for what have you that you can depend on*
> *more?*
> *A man's conscience can tell him his situation*
> *better than seven watchmen in a lofty tower.*
> *Most important of all, pray to God*
> *to set your feet in the path of truth.*
> *A word is the source of every deed,*
> *a thought, of every act.*
> *The root of all conduct is the mind,*

four branches it shoots forth;
good and evil, death and life,
their absolute mistress is the tongue.
(Sirach 37: 11-18)

Thank God that Lorraine and her family did not give up and stop praying. Thank God that Toby was there to help pray.

After we left the hospital, Lorraine got great news. A new prognosis was delivered. It was not what the doctors first thought. Now they found the problem to be lymphoma and it was treatable.

Ralph ended up having a miraculous recovery. Not because of any great faith I had, but because God wanted Lorraine and all of her family, too, understand how real He is. Now many years later, Ralph is still alive and well.

The words of wisdom from Sirach certainly fit in this case and they help me to understand that there will be no cowards in Heaven. Only people who believe every word of God, and put it into practice, will live with Jesus forever.

In this situation, I was operating out of pride and fear of failure. In working a miracle, you have to disassociate yourself from pride and become like a five-year-old child asking his father for a favor. Faith is paramount. You have to believe that the miracle is going to happen and drive the sin of doubt away.

Jesus, I pray for the gift of guarding my tongue well. Satan tries to use it as his tool every day. Jesus, please allow me to be a willing servant in all things. I am prone to failure when I operate without you. I need you with me at every moment of my life. Thank you, Jesus, for your advice, when you told the rich man to pray without ceasing. I see that when I don't listen to you, I fall into the evil one's traps.

The rain

In order for me to tell you the story of Jessica, I have to recount a story from my first book, "The Day the Rain Stopped." I want to do this because it shows how God works one miracle to set up the next.

We will go back to when I still worked at KDKA television and was trying to balance my life with work and prayer. I was going to Mass each day, saying the fifteen decades of the Rosary each day, fasting on bread and water on Wednesdays and Fridays, going to Confession each month and having conversion of the heart each day.

When I wasn't at the television station, I was working for God full-time. I had a tremendous idea (inspiration) of inviting people to come to my farm and pray for a whole day. I made plans to provide Mass, Stations of the Cross, fifteen decades of the Rosary, speakers, a bookstore, and a healing service. Also, because I thought this might be the first time many people were ever on a farm, I threw in a wiener roast.

Everyone at Gospa Missions helped to distribute flyers and we advertised the best we could with little or no money. Six hundred people signed up for this great day. Realizing that I could not accommodate six hundred people if it should rain, let alone have them all driving into the farm on a soupy, muddy farm road, I panicked a little. I went to John Loufman, our weather man at the television station, and asked him what the weather would be like the following Saturday. He explained that forecasting the weather a week away was a tough call, but not wanting to let me down, he invited me to the weather room to take a look.

"If I had to take a long shot I would say it was going to rain next Saturday," John said. "Come back in a few days and I will know better." The following Monday he stuck to his forecast of rain. On Wednesday, he stated that not only was it going to rain on Saturday, it was going to rain hard all day. It was going to rain all day Friday and all day Sunday. This wet weather front was not going away.

I don't know why I do some of the things I do, but just then, my right index finger jumped into John's face and these words came out of my mouth, "You watch the power of God, John, because it is not going to rain on my farm on Saturday." John Loufman laughed at me and walked away.

The big day finally came. Saturday! I got up in the morning and went outside. To my dismay, I found it raining hard. I looked up into the sky and spoke to God.

"Hey, God, You said if I wanted to move a mountain, I could, if I had enough faith. So I ask You, with the faith that You taught me to have, please stop this rain, part these skies and bring the sun out. There are six hundred people coming here to pray and they will not come if it is raining. Oh, and if You are going to do this, You will also need to bring a lot of wind because the road is all mud now and people will not be able to drive on the road to get to this farm."

That moment the rain ceased, the clouds rolled back, and the sun came out, and then the wind began to blow. In one hour the road was dry and people from all around the tri-state area came to the farm to pray. They all had the same words on their lips, "How could it be raining everywhere else but here?"

The miracles of that day continued and were profound, but the point of repeating this story here, as I said, was to show how God was setting John Loufman up for the story of his life. Let's jump forward to the following Monday when I met John in the hallway at work. When he saw me, John said, "It didn't rain on your farm on Saturday, did it?" "No, John, it didn't," I replied. John started to say, "That was the closest thing to a miracle I have ever seen." I interrupted, saying, "Not the closest thing to a miracle, John. It *was* a miracle." The hook was now set by God for John's journey with the Lord down the road.

Jessica

Later, after I had quit my job at the television station to give my life to Jesus, I lost track of all my friends at KDKA-TV, but God did not. One day John Loufman called. I had all but forgotten about him and most everyone else there. After a few brief exchanges, he asked, "Tom, are you still doing that God stuff?" Chuckling inside, I responded, "Yes, John, I'm still doing that God stuff."

After all that God has done for me, how could I stop? My conversion is now more than fourteen years old, through the grace of God, and I thank Him every day for it. But I know there were many, including my wife, who were waiting for me to give it up. I guess John was hoping I hadn't.

John Loufman was calling because he had a very big problem in his life. He had an eight-year-old niece, Jessica, who was dying of leukemia. John explained that she contracted Hodgkins disease but the medical community had been successful in defeating it. In the process, the doctors had to give Jessica many radiation treatments. The Hodgkins disease was eradicated, but as a result of all the radiation she received, Jessica contracted leukemia. With radiation being the recommended treatment for leukemia, the doctors were now in a dilemma. If they didn't treat Jessica with radiation, she would surely die. But if they gave her more radiation, they predicted that it would probably kill her. It appeared that there was nothing else the doctors could do for little Jessica.

Maybe the doctors used the stock line, "It is in God's hands now." What people do not understand is that it is always in God's hands, so why not start there?

John asked, because of his recollection of God and the rainy day, if I would pray for Jessica. "Not only will I pray for Jessica," I said to John, "tell me where she is and I will come to visit her."

I know prayer, combined with a personal visit, is many times more powerful than prayer alone. I understand the faith of the centurion in Scripture, but I also believe God honors all of our efforts. If the Lord sees our wanting to set our own lives aside to help another human being, then that adds to the power of the prayer. There are many things that add to the power of prayer, such as your faith - simply believing with all your heart that it will work. Fasting is another tremendous boost to seeing prayers answered and other aids that we will cover later.

John explained that Jessica was in the Cleveland Clinic in Ohio. This hospital was about three hours away from me and it was possible to get there, so I made arrangements to meet John the following day. I also told him to get as many people as possible to pray and fast for her. I mentioned the Rosary and he explained that neither he nor his sister, the child's mother, were Catholic. "Then say prayers you know," I told him. He agreed to get the ball rolling and we hung up.

I asked Toby Gaines to go with me again and being the good Catholic that he is, his answer was yes. The next morning we set off for Cleveland. Scripture says, *"Where two or more are gathered, there am I in their midst."* With three hours of the driving time available, we used it to our advantage to prepare for the work to come. We said the Rosary. Not one-third of a Rosary, but we said it all - the Joyful, Sorrowful and Glorious Mysteries. We, through the Rosary, relived the life, death and resurrection of Jesus. And we said it slowly. It is better to say one Our Father slowly, than to rush through a full fifteen decades of the Rosary.

When we got to the hospital, John took us to Jessica's room to meet her. Once there, we found out how much of an impact Jessica had on everyone. They all loved her at the hospital. The nurses were commenting on what a great patient Jessica was. She was a vibrant young girl and quite talented. Her art work, a large mural, was displayed in the hall.

I then had a talk with Jessica, a real heart-to-heart talk. I told her how I worked for God and, at times, when I prayed for sick people, they got well. Included in my explanation was that the prayers didn't always work the way we thought and hoped they would, but I needed her help to increase the chances. I explained that she had to believe that God would help her. I introduced her to Toby and said he was there to help her, too.

Then we laid hands on Jessica's head and said individually, "I bless you with the blessing of Blessed Mother and may the power of the Holy Spirit come upon you." "That's it," I told her. "That is all that we have to say in the way of a prayer," but I also told her I would go to Mass every day for her and say the Rosary and fast for her. Not a bad gift from someone you just met. Not a bad gift for anyone with any problem in the world. It is the most powerful combination in existence. The only thing more I could do was to increase the frequency of my prayer and fasting and leave it up to the will of God.

We returned home. A few days later I got a call from John Loufman telling me how everything in little Jessica's body changed the day we prayed for her. All of the indicators that the doctors track from their tests had changed from the level that said Jessica was dying to a level that would allow them to give her a bone marrow transplant. There was now new hope! Scripture says, "This kind [the more difficult cases] takes much prayer and much fasting." That is exactly what we all needed to do - pray and fast for continued success.

John would call from time to time to give me reports on Jessica's progress and I would pray and fast. The little girl was sent off to a new kind of bone marrow transplant center. At the center they tried to find a match for her bone marrow, but a good match was not found and time was running out again. John called and with some panic in his voice, was asking for more fervent prayer. It was time to do the transplant, match or no match. It was Jessica's only chance, the doctors said.

It was not always easy for John to find me because of my constant traveling throughout the world evangelizing. In the next call I received from John, the panic in his voice seemed to have increased considerably. I soon found out why. The transplant had failed and the bone marrow was being rejected by Jessica's body. "Please," John said. "Pray harder."

At this point I addressed Jesus about the problem. "Lord, You said we could ask anything of the Father in Your name and it would be granted. So I am begging on behalf of Jessica and her family. Please help them again." An answer came to me instantly. *"She is already healed, Thomas. Have faith."* I had faith. What I didn't have was the guts to tell John that Jesus said Jessica was already healed. What if she died after I said she would live? That would make me a false prophet. I decided I would rather not be a prophet at all, so I said nothing.

The next call I got from John (and he had to find me on the road again) was a call of despair. "Tom, the doctors have told us to call the family and friends in and say good-bye to Jessica. They say she has only two days to live. And they want her parents to tell Jessica that she has only two days left, that she has a right to know." What a horrible feeling came over me. I panicked, too, but not over Jessica's dying. I knew that wasn't going to happen or I wasn't really dealing with Jesus. Panic came over me just thinking about what an awful thing it would be for Jessica to hear the words, "You only have two days to live."

"Please, John, do not tell that little girl that she is going to be dead in two days. That isn't true. I am sorry that I was too much a coward to say anything before, but Jesus told me that she is going to live. Where is Jessica right now? I will go to her." John informed me that Jessica was in the Fred Hutchinson Cancer Research Center in Seattle, Washington. Astonished is the only word that I can use to describe the way I felt at that moment. Mary and I were in Seattle, Washington! John gave me the address and room number, and off we went to Hutchinson Cancer Center.

When we got to Jessica's room, I greeted her parents. This was maybe only the third time that I had ever met them. They filled us in on what had been occurring and they told us how hard they had been praying. Then I walked over to see Jessica. I felt faint. This little girl had changed so dramatically. She was transformed from a beautiful little girl to a little person who looked like death was about to visit. She was so yellow all over and black and blue in many places. There were tubes in her mouth and nose. I could see that Jessica was having a hard time breathing. It is a moment that can make a person ask God, "Why?"

Recovering instantly, and knowing that this was not a moment for doubt, I said to Jessica's mother, "Jessica is going to be okay." My hand went on the little girl's frail head and I said for the second time, "I bless you with the blessing of the Blessed Mother and may the power of the Holy Spirit come upon you." I took my hand off her head and turned to those in the room and I said, "I realize that some of you are Protestant, but pray this prayer with me." And I started. "Hail Mary, full of grace, the Lord is with you. Blessed are you among women and blessed is the fruit of your womb, Jesus. Holy Mary, Mother of God, pray for us sinners, now and at the hour of our death. Amen."

That was all we could do. It had really been in God's hands the entire time. This had been a test for all of us, but now it seemed that the test was over. We said our good-byes and we were off. I had to go back and do the other job for which God had sent me to Seattle - speak to a group of Catholics.

John called several times to tell me how, all of a sudden, Jessica started to respond after I left. She got better and better each day, according to the messages I received from John. Soon Jessica was released from the hospital and went home. I have never seen Jessica since that day. The last time I called to check on her, she was too busy to come to the phone to talk to me. It seems Jessica was out in the woods with her dad, building a shack.

Many doctors worked very hard to save Jessica's life. They used equipment that cost millions of dollars. The hospital bills had to have been staggering and yet they failed. Their system declared that Jessica would die in two days. Didn't happen. Most certainly, Jessica will die; we all do. But it will happen when God decides that it's time.

In this case, God wanted to use me, a man who lied to get out of high school, who sinned in a big way and didn't go to church for twenty-seven years. I believe God wanted to show people that He can change anyone and then give that person a job in the vineyard. He worked through me and all of the others who prayed and fasted to heal Jessica. That does not make us heroes. No! It makes us tools in God's hand.

If doctors only could see their way clear to combining their skills with the power of the Holy Spirit, we would see much more in the way of medical successes. Prayer and fasting are the keys. Service to the Lord is the answer to everything.

Chapter Five

Express Lane

Father Jozo

Today God will work miracles through any of us if we become willing participants. I was in the habit of visiting Father Jozo, a Franciscan priest from Bosnia, in his hometown of Tihaljina. Perhaps around the sixth or seventh visit I made to see him and hear one of his talks, I became truly amazed how the reputation of this very charismatic priest had spread worldwide. Father Jozo's homilies were profound, even through a translator. They taught a Catholic faith that was not some "watered down" version. His homilies were the kind that John the Baptizer would deliver if he were alive today.

Father Jozo also prayed over people by laying his hand on their head. Many people, when touched by him, were rendered unconscious through the power of the Holy Spirit. There were many spiritual and physical healings through him. Because of this, the groups coming to his church were getting larger and larger.

Father Jozo was imprisoned by the Communist government around 1981 and suffered much for the Catholic faith. Maybe this is why the Spirit of God worked through him in such a powerful way.

Regarding the supernatural and the miraculous, Father Jozo is well-informed. Nevertheless, great people, even famous priests like Father Jozo, sometimes have a loss of faith for a brief moment and lose sight of the belief that all is possible with God.

I remember a day when the crowd was so large at Father Jozo's church that, after his talk, he announced that he was not going to be laying his hands on people's heads and blessing them. He made the statement because, in his opinion, there were just too many people. When he made that announcement, a sinking feeling raced through my heart. I knew how much everybody in my own pilgrimage group was looking forward to receiving his blessing.

As he announced the words, I did not even need a second to think. I caught sight of the statue of the Sacred Heart of Jesus positioned just to the right of the altar. I ran over, dropped to my knees in front of the statue, and I started begging Jesus to change Father's mind. He had already begun walking away. "Please, Jesus," I begged, "change his heart, change his mind. You know how everybody loves this blessing. Please change his heart."

Instantly, Father Jozo turned around and came back to the microphone and said, "I have changed my mind." He was going to do the blessing! The joy that filled my heart was profound, first to know that everyone was going to receive this special blessing and second to know how quickly God will answer a prayer.

Father Jozo has to work very hard when he prays over people. It takes many hours for him to pray over a large crowd. The reason I know how difficult it is for him is because, in my ministry, I also go out and lay on hands and I pray over people. I was inspired by him to do it. Quite often, if there are hundreds of people in a church, your arms become very tired because you must hold them up for a long time. Your muscles start to ache and the pain becomes intense. At that point, I always make a request of God. "If you give me the grace, I will stay and pray over these people all night." The grace comes and the job gets done. So I realize why Father Jozo was so willing to set aside the blessing that day, but I thank God for the gift we all received when the miracle happened.

I went back to visit Father Jozo about a month later. The crowd must have doubled in size. I marveled at how many people were there. The church was filled to over-flowing. Once again, Father Jozo delivered a dynamic talk that shot right into everybody's heart. People were changing right before our very eyes. At the end of the talk, he again apologized to everyone and said that bless-ing everyone would be impossible because of the large number of people.

One could see that he felt badly about not giving the blessing. I could hear the sighs from the crowd. As Father Jozo started to walk away, I, with the cocky attitude that still sneaks up on me sometimes, addressed the problem with the Lord again. This time my reaction was not to run up in front of the Sacred Heart of Jesus. This time I just said, "Lord, do we have to go through this again? Here, sitting in the pews of this church, are many priests who would jump at the chance to help. Father Jozo can bless these priests with his special blessing and then all of the priests can help bless all the people." Father Jozo turned around instantly and stepped back up to the microphone and said, "I have changed my mind. Will all the priests present please come forward?"

I tell you that it is the power of prayer! When it is a selfless prayer, God wants to answer that prayer. He is hungering to answer prayers. You might say that you pray, but perhaps the trouble is that your prayers may be more on the order of asking (or even demanding!) that He do something *for you*, fix something *for you* or provide something *for you*. We are trying to make God the servant. He is not the servant. He is the Master. We are the servants. My begging was in behalf of the thousand or more people there. "Please Lord, *they need* this grace," I prayed. God then changed Father Jozo's heart, so that many miracles would occur that afternoon.

The really fascinating part about this little drama I have just related is that Father Jozo never knew he was manipulated by prayer. He probably thinks he just changed his own mind.

The Spirit moves me

We have moved Gospa Missions from our original storefront location at 121 East Main Street in Evans City, Pennsylvania, up the block to 230 East Main. When the Lord had me move Gospa Missions from my house and put us in that first building in the heart of our little town, it seemed to be a crazy plan. The building was too large. We were lost in all that space. It was 2400 square feet. Three years later, the Mission had grown so much and we had so many volunteers, we were out of space. Now God was urging me to move again. I started to look for a new location.

In the end, we purchased the largest building in Evans City, renovating it and turning it into the nicest building in Evans City. Now we have more than three times the space. There were many frustrating moments in that first building because of our rapid growth. "Stuff" became piled up everywhere. There wasn't a square inch that was not used.

Another frustration in the first building was its location. It was only three doors down from the railroad tracks. You could throw a stone and hit the tracks from our front door. Although the trains slow down a bit when they come through the town, they still shake everything as they rumble along. It wasn't terrible, but the pictures on the wall would always be hanging a little crooked after a train would pass. They came through as many as ten times a day. To let the traffic know that the train was coming, the engineer would blow his horn. A very loud horn. At first the loud sound was aggravating for us, but after a year or so, we hardly noticed it.

One day while I was working in my office at the old Gospa Missions, I heard the horn of a train. It wasn't unlike any of the other horns on the trains passing through town, but this particular sound caused me to react in a very strange way. I jumped up from my seat and ran outside, looking to the east, toward the tracks. I could see cars backed up from the traffic light and they were strung out beyond the tracks. One driver had the car parked right on the tracks while waiting for a traffic light to change. What a stupid thing to do!

The horn grew louder as the train was getting closer. The driver was not moving the car. I started to run toward the car yelling, "Get off the tracks!" I was motioning for the cars in front of the one on the tracks to pull up to give this car room to move forward. As I approached the car on the tracks, I now could see that it was a woman behind the wheel. I also could hear that she was playing the radio very loudly and that made her oblivious to the train horn. She had no idea that a train was coming.

I started beating on her window with my fist to get her attention. The only thing that could have scared her more was if the arm of the crossing gate that closes off the intersection would have hit her car. The train was approaching the intersection and the engineer was laying on the horn. The arm of the crossing gate was lowering. I was yelling, "Get off the tracks! Get off the tracks!" as I was pointing toward the train. Finally realizing what was going on, the woman stepped on the accelerator. The car raced forward as the crossing arm just squeaked past her trunk. I ran from the track area and the train came rumbling through, the wheels screeching and the horn blasting. My heart was pounding. In a moment, the light changed and I am almost sure the woman never realized that she came close to dying.

God had just spared that woman's life by prompting me, for no earthly reason, to go out and look toward the tracks. God came to her aid in the second that she needed Him. We never realize how many times God intervenes in our lives, how He sends someone at just the right moment. We live our lives as though we are invincible and we are not. We think we have lots of time to square things up with the Lord. We tell ourselves we will change later, maybe tomorrow. But Jesus comes like a thief in the night. You have to be ready. **Today**.

Thomas Rutkoski

Chapter Six

The Blessing

When I lay my hand on someone's head, I say, "I bless you with the blessing of the Blessed Mother and may the power of the Holy Spirit come upon you."

The explanation of how I received and began to use this blessing is rather humorous and is contained in my first book.

Interestingly enough, each person who receives this blessing can then pass it on. It becomes more powerful the more often it is used. What makes it really powerful is going to Mass each day, saying fifteen decades of the Rosary each day, and fasting on bread and water on Wednesdays and Fridays. (Is this beginning to sound familiar?)

Many times people relate that when my hand touches their head, they feel a tremendous warmth pass through them. Others say they feel something like electricity all through them. Children, I notice, often start to twitch, and there is a very obvious shifting their bodies, not done on their own.

With my hand on someone's head, I sometimes feel a cracking or shifting of their skull. This process obviously doesn't hurt or they would say something.

91

I, on the other hand, at times have felt great pain as I give the blessing. One time, in someone's house in Colorado, I experienced what I can only describe as a heart attack. Without taking my right hand off the man for whom I was praying, my left hand clutched at my chest. It was very difficult to breathe and the pain was crushing. Afterwards, one person asked why I had gripped my chest the way I did. I told him of my experience and he explained that the man for whom I was praying at the time the pain had come over me had been diagnosed with a bad heart condition and had to go to the hospital soon. I don't know what happened to him after I left.

I usually ask God to wait until I leave town before He works any of His great miracles because I don't want to be blamed for them. I don't know if the man recovered from his heart problem, but surely God wasn't wasting our time.

That same night, as I closed my eyes and prayed for a woman, suddenly I could see a priest standing in front of me. I finished praying, opened my eyes and took my hand off her head. I rarely speak to people when I pray for them and I prefer that people don't speak to me. I'm not intending to be arrogant when I say that. If people start to explain their conditions, I inform them that God already knows their problems. So, in contrast to my usual procedure, to this woman I said, "Do you have a priest in your family?" She replied, "Yes, my son is a priest. Why do you ask?" "Oh, never mind. I just wondered." We may never know or understand why God chooses to provide us with these little insights. Let's just be glad that He does.

Chuck Hantusch

Chuck's story is just one of many of this sort. Chuck was our sales representative for the company, Knepper Press, that prints our newsletter. He became a good friend to some of us at Gospa Missions. He had been very affected by reading my first book. He said it changed his life very much.

Chuck came to me one day at Gospa Missions. It was obvious that he had something serious on his mind. I could see it in his face. I asked what the problem was and he explained that he had been going to the doctor and just received some bad news. The doctor had just informed him that he had prostate cancer.

That is something one normally tells close friends, but in this case, Chuck wasn't telling me just for the sake of my knowing. He wanted me to do something about it. He had read in my book that I prayed for the sick and recalled reading that sometimes the sick get well because of my prayers.

It is strange to have people come to me with these kinds of problems and expect results. Is that not what doctors are for? How much logic is there in going to some-one like myself, who lied to get out of high school, rather than going to a doctor who probably has a minimum of seven years of post-collegiate education? In worldly terms, there is no logic in that. But this has nothing to do with worldly logic. This has more to do with faith.

Chuck was reaching out to God through another human being. You could wonder, "Why not simply ask God Himself?" Knowing the state of his relationship with God and reading about mine, Chuck analyzed the situation. He knew he didn't do all that I claimed I did in my relationship with God. Surely he was prompted by the Holy Spirit to relate his problem to me. Drastic measures for serious situations, perhaps. Get all of the help you can is good advice. As things turned out, it was the Holy Spirit leading Chuck to God's way of doing things.

What do *you* do when one of your friends comes to you with bad news in his or her life? Do you say, "I'm sorry," or "Oh, how awful?" How about considering what I did when Chuck told me his bad news? He came in faith and asked for my prayers because he believed in what he had read. The stories in the book had touched his heart. God was work.

I told him to lean over so I could lay my hand on his head. Chuck leaned over and I placed my hand lightly on his head and prayed, "I bless you with the blessing of the Blessed Mother and may the power of the Holy Spirit come upon you."

It seems to be an awfully simple formula for curing prostate cancer, does it not? Well, it is not as simple a formula as it may seem at first. I back up this one-on-one prayer with my entire life. I quit my job for the Lord and now go town to town all over the world trying to find his lost sheep. I go to Mass every day and pray fifteen decades of the Rosary most days. I fast on bread and water on Wednesdays and Fridays and a whole lot more.

The end result was that Chuck came to visit me again several days later. With tears in his eyes he tried to explain that when he went back to his doctors, they found nothing wrong with him. They said they must have made a mistake. I think not!

If I can lay my life down, you can also. There is no difference between us. I was a hunter, fisherman, golfer, boater and the list goes on. It isn't what we are, it is what we can be. If you give your life to the Lord, you will be able to help people who come to you.

It is a shame that more people cannot bring themselves to believe that God really does send these kinds of gifts through common people. The greatest shame of all is that some religious do not encourage the flock to lead lives that would produce fruit of this kind. Oh, yes, they read the Scriptures that explain that these are the kinds of charisms which accompany the followers of Jesus, but they let it go at merely reading it. I have encountered only a few priests in all these years who, upon finishing a passage on this subject, genuinely encouraged their congregations to go out and try to become like the apostles, to use the gifts that Jesus had given them. We are so willing to relegate Jesus' instructions for gaining His favor to having meaning only in a faraway place nearly two-thousand years ago. Not true! If we don't apply the Scriptures to our lives every day, they become nothing more than a collection of stories. Was divine inspiration provided for so trivial a purpose?

If our priests, who are on the front lines, only had the prayer and fasting support from the congregation, they would be able to teach the kind of life-style it takes to be a true follower of Jesus. Our paths would be so much clearer. Not easier, mind you, clearer.

Please, Fathers, believe in who you are. I will pray and fast for you and will gather as many as I can to do the same. I am sorry that I let you down for so many years. I now understand and accept my responsibility of being Catholic.

To you good priests who love the Church and follow the Magisterium, may God continue to bless you. Thank you for teaching me to do it God's way. Thank you for being a priest and giving your life to God.

We all need to give our lives to God. In treating God far too casually, we see very few spiritual fruits. The story of Chuck Hantusch can and should be played out in all of our lives. It would happen if we decide today to take God seriously.

The woman on crutches

Mary and I drove to Windsor, Ontario, Canada. The kind people at Assumption Church invited me to speak there. I was at the back of the church distributing the Gospa Missions newsletter and greeting people as they arrived. Mary was setting up our traveling bookstore. At many of my presentations, we sell religious products to help support our apostolate. It was an evening just like all the rest. Some people came desiring a healing. A few people came in wheelchairs or on crutches. Generally, word gets around that I pray over each person that comes to the presentation and, at times, people are healed.

I know from lessons taught to me by the Lord that a miracle on the body is only a manifestation of Divine Power. The saving of souls is the work of Jesus Christ. He works miracles to get our attention. Not only the attention of the person who receives the miracle, but for all who witness the miracle or hear about it. This is so we may believe, learn and then put the Word of God into practice.

This night I must have been in a fairly lighthearted mood because, as a younger woman hobbled past me on crutches, going into the church, I jokingly said, "Hey, lady, no running in here." She got the joke. She turned, smiled and said, "No, sir, I won't be doing any running." She continued on to take her seat in the church.

97

After everyone was seated, I delivered my presentation. I don't remember what the subject was that night, but I always pull from the vast assortment of gifts the Lord has given to me or to someone through me. I never go to a church with notes or even a preconceived notion of what I will talk about. I leave it up to the Holy Spirit. After my talk, as usual, I explained that little blessing that I was going to give everyone. At that point, I invited them all forward to receive it.

That night, there were perhaps four-hundred people in the church. Eventually my hand rested on the head of the woman with the crutches, the one with whom I joked. I gave her the blessing and as I took my hand off her head, one of the rare instances of my speaking to someone during the blessing happened. I said, still in a joking way, "You can go outside and run now." I then continued with the blessings for everyone remaining.

After the last person was blessed and the lights were being turned out, a woman came running back into the church. In a very excited way she said, "Hey, mister! You know the lady you prayed for?" I asked, "What lady? I prayed for a lot of people tonight." She answered excitedly, "The one on the crutches! The one you told to go outside and run now."

"Oh, yes, I remember her," I said. "Well!" she exclaimed, "She is out in the parking lot doing that and they can't get her stopped!"

At that point, a man came running into the church. He grabbed me and started hugging me and said, "You healed my daughter . . . you healed my daughter . . . thank you!" "No, sir," I advised the man. "I didn't heal your daughter. Jesus Christ healed your daughter. Go and thank Jesus."

It is a fact. I cannot heal anyone. However, if we say yes to Jesus, He can get a lot done in this world through us. And obviously, He did that night.

Father William Kiel

I was leading a pilgrimage overseas in November, 1994, and a priest, Father William Kiel, accompanied us as a spiritual director. We had a seven-hour layover at the Frankfurt airport in Germany. At the airport chapel, there was a Mass being said and we all attended. It was kind of neat to have a Catholic chapel inside an airport. After the Mass, I gave about an hour-long talk. I figured I would consume some time, so that everyone wasn't too bored waiting for the next flight.

After the talk, Father Kiel asked, "Tom, could I say something to the people?" I replied, "Of course, Father, that's why you are along, to encourage and help these people." He got up in front of everyone and revealed, "I've only been a priest for about a year and a half now." He went on to tell his miraculous story:

[The following is the personal testimony of Father William Kiel, then-pastor of Saint Mary of Guadalupe Church in Kittanning, Pennsylvania. He is currently pastor of St. John the Evangelist in Uniontown, PA. I believe it shows how each of us, as lay people, can have a profound effect in this world, in the name of God.]

For twenty-three years, I, William Kiel, taught high school biology. I was teaching in a public high school. In 1985 I started to think seriously about the priesthood. I was always a religiously-oriented person, but now, at the age of forty-two, I realized that there was a definite calling, a tugging on my heart, so to speak. At Greensburg Salem High School, where I taught, there was a teacher's strike. It lasted from November 1985, to January 1986. I thought, "This is not for me." "This is not the kind of life I want to live, as a teacher." I started praying and thinking about the priesthood. A year and a half later, I looked into the priesthood with a vocational director. Eighteen months later, I was in the seminary.

During the time I was teaching biology, I was very involved with the Church. I taught religious education classes, was a Eucharistic minister, and was on the parish council. I thought, if I decide to be a priest, this involvement in the Church would give me a unique perspective. I'll be able to look at the Church as both priest and lay person.

Sure enough, it helped tremendously, because today, I am a priest. When I thought seriously about the priesthood, I went into the seminary. When the decision was final, I attended St. Vincent Seminary in Latrobe, Pennsylvania. St.Vincent is a school that is conducted by the Benedictines, a great order of priests.

In the seminary, I prayed for direction for my vocation. I also prayed that God would help and heal me. From about 1976 on, I had a back injury which left me in constant pain. I went to chiropractors and to neurosurgeons, but to no avail. I had a lot of problems with pain. There were days spent teaching that I would have to leave school to go to the chiropractor.

In February of my third year at St.Vincent, I went to the nearby town of Mt. Pleasant for my brother's birthday dinner. While there, he said to me, "You know, you're in the seminary now, and there is a man speaking at the church . . . I think his name is Rutkoski. It's a good Polish name and you are part Polish. Why don't you go with me to listen to him speak? He is supposed to have a good message."

My brother and I went, and we listened. After his talk, we were left with a great impression of Tom Rutkoski, who spoke of his conversion. After Tom was finished speaking, he invited all of us to the front of the church for a blessing. I was sitting in a pew about halfway back and from my position, I watched these people being blessed. Some of them started to fall, but recovered. Some ended up on the floor, seemingly unconscious.

My first thought was,"Wait a minute. This guy can't bless people. He is only a lay person. This can't be happening in the Catholic Church! You only see this on television. You only see this with Protestant evangelists and it always looked so fake. They must hit the people on the head to cause them to fall back."

With Tom, though, he would just lay his hand on the person's head, what seemed to be ever so lightly, and the person would fall over. I asked what was happening and was told they were "resting in the Spirit." I thought, "Whoa, as a Catholic seminarian, what should I do? Should I go up there for that blessing or should I just let other people go? Should I report this man to the Church? What should I do?"

I started praying to the Holy Spirit. "If this is of You, Holy Spirit, let me be open to receiving the blessing and whatever happens, happens." The next thing I knew, I was walking up to get my blessing. Tom laid his hand on my head so gently. He said, "I bless you with the blessing of the Blessed Mother, and may the power of the Holy Spirit come upon you." I wobbled a little bit and almost fell over, but I caught myself. Tom then put his hands back on my head and started to thank Jesus. At that point I was gone. I guess I was "resting in the Spirit."

I don't know how long I lay on the floor unconscious. When I got up, I started to walk back to my pew. The only way I can explain what started to happen to me is that it was a feeling that I had never had before. It was like I was walking, my legs were moving, but I couldn't touch the floor. It was astounding! It didn't feel like my feet were touching the floor. When I made it back to the pew, I experienced complete peace. It was a feeling that I have not felt previously. It was then I realized that all of my back pain was gone. After that, my brother and I left the church.

Having grown up in the town of Mt. Pleasant, a lot of people who were in the church knew me. They knew I was in the seminary and they came to me and said, "Bill, what is this? What's going on here? We have never seen this happen in the Catholic Church." All I could say was, "Are you open to the Holy Spirit? Do you let the Holy Spirit work in your life? Just pray to be open and you will understand. You will experience something unique, something new." Afterwards, we left and went back to my brother's house. I said to my brother, Tom, "You know, I don't have any more back pain. It is all gone!" What do you do but thank God?

That was the first time I had my faith strengthened completely by a physical miracle. Before this miracle, in the seminary, I kept praying that God would take care of my back. I knew by the way I suffered that I could not stand at an altar for an hour. I was always wondering how I was going to become a priest with all of this pain. I had to be moving constantly, and at Mass, you can't do that. Sure enough, my prayer was answered at a time and in a way I did not expect. I had a tiny bit of stiffness left, but no pain at all.

All of that strengthened me for the priesthood. It strengthened me for a time when I would be able to go out and tell my parishioners and all people that there is a God, there is a Holy Spirit, and *miracles do happen*. I am a living example of it.

A few months later, I attended a talk given by a Father DiOrio at the Convention Center in Pittsburgh. I was still in the seminary at the time. I went there to serve as a Eucharistic minister. After Father was finished with his talk, he asked everyone to form a circle inside of the Convention Center, so that he could give us a blessing. I got a blessing from Father DiOrio and again, "rested in the Spirit."

Following that talk, I went to a nursing home to visit my mother. I was telling her about my experiences. I said, "Mom, I got that blessing from a man by the name of Thomas Rutkoski. When he touched me, I was rendered unconscious. When I got up, my back was completely healed. After that, I still had some stiffness in my back, but then I realized, as I moved, that I didn't even feel the stiffness. Then, last night, I had the opportunity to hear Father DiOrio and again, after a blessing, I "rested in the Spirit." Now I am not even the slightest bit stiff.

You know, as priests, we give blessings to many people. However, we don't take the time to get blessings for the strength that we ourselves need. Whenever I get the opportunity, as I did with Tom and Father DiOrio, I will again receive the gifts that God offers and be strengthened through blessings.

Another note about myself: I went on a pilgrimage to Bosnia with Tom Rutkoski. I was not really expecting anything, but just being open to everything that could be going on there. In fact, a number of great things did happen there. One of them occurred when we went to listen to a priest named Father Jozo. Three priests and a deacon celebrated Mass. After the Mass, Father Jozo came out and said something in Croatian and we were sitting there waiting for the interpreter. While he was talking, I was thinking, "This Father Jozo is telling the people that he is going to bless the three priests and he is going to ask them to bless the people in the church. Then I thought, I don't understand Croatian and that is even silly to think that I could understand him.

When he was finished, the interpreter said, "Father Jozo is going to bless these three priests. He is going to ask them to pass this blessing onto all the people, starting with the people in this church." I thought, "This is too good to be true." He then blessed us. After that, he motioned for us priests to go to a number of people in the Church. I blessed the people, as I saw Tom Rutkoski do. I laid my hands on their head. The people started to "rest in the Spirit." As I was doing this I thought, "I don't know what is happening, but then I didn't give it any more thought. I continued to put my hands on the people's heads and pray for them. When I give the blessing, I don't see faces. I was praying for their souls.

When I finished with the line of people and looked back, I saw the people getting off the floor. People came up to me and said, "I thank you for the blessing. I think I have received a healing." I said, "Don't thank me; thank God. All I did was pray for you. I prayed to God for you."

As I made this statement, I remembered what we were taught in the seminary, "We do nothing as priests but pray for the people. God does the work. God leads us." How many times had I thought of that statement, but never really felt the impact? A greater realization of that very teaching is the fact that I received another healing the same day through Father Jozo. I had bad migraine headaches for years and can only figure that they left through his blessing because I have not had one since.

Since that time I have shared that blessing and prayed for many people with great results, (great the healings.) There were not only physical healings, but more importantly, spiritual healings and peace of heart, most certainly a peace that those affected had never felt before. It was a peace that they never had with their God before. Once we have that peace, we have that love, we want to share that peace and love with others.

So many times we are told that if we don't have love, we cannot give it away. The more love you have, the more love you give away, and the more love you receive. God is just waiting to give you love, so you can give it to others. God works through us, every one of us (priests and laity alike). It is only with your cooperation that the work of God can spread. Always remember that you are Christ to others.

When Christ left this earth at the Ascension, He left us behind to be His hands, to be His feet, to be His lips. Then, on Pentecost, He left us the Holy Spirit to guide us in becoming "Christlike." If we can only remember that when we are "Christlike" we have the love of Christ and the love of God within us, and we will want to give it to others. We will want to pray to the Father for others. We will want to lead others to

God. That is why we are all here. Also, as baptized Catholics, we are responsible for leading others to God.

As a perfect example, God gave us the Blessed Mother. She leads us to her Son. Who better than a mother knows how to reach her children? The Blessed Mother leads us, guides us, and strengthens us so that we may be aware of Jesus Christ and of God the Father. The role of the Blessed Mother is to help to get us to where we need to be for salvation. Our Blessed Mother is always interceding for us. We wouldn't have as many of these miracles, like the one I received, if it were not for the Blessed Mother. She gave us Jesus. All the prayers to the Blessed Mother, all the shrines to the Blessed Mother, wouldn't be there if they weren't important.

The Blessed Mother's blessing changed my life. It is the reason I am a priest today. Thank God!

[*This is the end of Father Kiel's testimony.*]

We have just seen that God used me, the great sinner, Thomas Rutkoski, to heal a man so he could become a priest. If God will work through me, He will work through you. We have to get this in our heads. God wants to do great things through us. We've got to become willing participants. We've got to be able to say, "Yes, here I am Lord. I have come to do Your will." When you start backing that with the message of prayer and fasting, then life doesn't become boring. Life with God is extremely exciting.

Many people are afraid of God. A hymn I truly love proclaims, "Be not afraid!" There is nothing to fear. God loves us! Turn toward Him. Give Him all your mind, all your heart, all your soul, all your strength, and pray without ceasing. This cannot be considered a boring concept. This opens doors to the miraculous. Then, all of a sudden, life is worth living.

I have always loved traveling. In my case, I thought that once I went to work for God that my traveling days would be over and I would miss out on all of that excitement. Wrong! God is traveling me to death! I have been all over the world through the grace of God! One of my greatest desires was to tour all of America. Well! I have not only been all over North America, but I have experienced the South Pacific, Asia, Africa, South America and Europe as well. If intelligent life is discovered on other planets, I would hope to be sent there also, to tell them about Jesus Christ Who saved me. This God stuff is great! It's exciting every single day.

Thomas Rutkoski

Chapter Seven

Attacks by Satan

Our God is so good. Once you get on His side and go to work for Him, life becomes a lot of fun. God Himself is a lot of fun and He has a sense of humor. He converted me! Ask anybody who knew me B.C. (before Christ), and they will laugh. God converted *whom*?

I don't want to lead you down a primrose path by telling you that, if you turn your life over to God, all is going to be well. It probably will not. In fact, when you turn your life over to God, your life, to the worldly people around you, will not seem like fun. Remember that you have to become *not of this world*. Nothing that happens to you on earth, if you do it God's way, will make sense to those around you. Many people, and even some religious, will think you have gone mad as you relate your Godly experiences. Unfortunately, there are not many people left who truly believe in God. That makes the whole world mission territory!

As you turn your life over to the will of the Father, He automatically becomes more believable. It is almost like the law of physical science: for every action there is an opposite and equal reaction. Except with God, that reaction is times ten. If you allow yourself, you will start to understand God's plan in your life. This is a good

111

place to inject a quote from Mother Teresa, "If you want to make God laugh, tell Him **your** plans."

Simultaneously, Satan will also become a reality in your life. Oh, he was there all the time, but now you will experience him firsthand. As long as people remain in a lukewarm state, Satan has no need to intervene. You truly belong to him. However, once you start a sincere journey toward holiness, look out. All Hell will break loose, if you know what I mean. Satan gets very upset if he is about to lose one of his disciples. He will try every day, all day long, to prevent the loss of your soul from his domain.

God allows Satan's attacks to test us and to make us strong. Much is accomplished in surviving trials and tribulations. It is when you persevere in these trials that you grow closer to God. Yes, it is then that you, too, will experience the miraculous, saving power of Jesus Christ.

Windswept feathers

Many times, when Satan attacks, he is relentless. People start to say all kinds of bad things about you. Charges are made against you; accusations and stories are concocted, and even your friends are willing to "hang you out to dry." So what! Just recognize them for what they are (attacks). Sometimes they can even get funny.

One day, Don Gaus, a wonderful friend who helped me build Gospa Missions to what it is today, came to me and said, "Hey, Tom, Father mentioned your name in church the other day." With great delight (expecting it to be something nice), I said, "Oh, what did he say?" I was really excited. "He said that you had a nervous breakdown and that people should probably stay away from you for a while." I exclaimed, "Get out of here!" He responded, "No, I'm serious, you ought to call him." I said, "You're pulling my leg." He said, "No, call him." Rising to the challenge, I said, "Okay, I will!" I figured he would stop me before I dialed, but he didn't, and I dialed. A priest then came to the phone.

"Father, this is Tom Rutkoski. I understand that you mentioned my name in church the other day." He replied, "Yeah! How are you doing, Tom?" He sounded solicitous. I responded in a kind and loving way, "Well, a better question than that is, if you wanted to know how I was doing, why didn't you call me? What is it that you actually said about me?" The priest explained, "I told people that you'd had a nervous breakdown and maybe we ought to back off a little bit. You are probably under a lot of pressure." I said, "How is it that you know that this is true?" He told me that he heard it from a very reliable source. Obviously, he did not! I asked him if I sounded like someone who had a nervous breakdown and Father said no. Then I said to the priest, "Father, Satan tries to kill me every day of my life."

Satan's point here was to destroy my reputation and to get me to become angry. I informed Father that Satan was not going to accomplish either of those objectives

113

this time. In this highly unfair and potentially very damaging situation, I actually kept my cool. That is not always the case.

"Do you understand what Satan accomplished here, Father? You announced to six hundred people. . . ." Before I finished, he interrupted anxiously, "Oh, no, I am going to tell them this Sunday that I was wrong and we are going to fix this."

I said, "It can't be fixed, Father! You told six hundred people and they have already gone out and told ten people each and now six thousand people have heard this untruth. Then this story spreads even more and then they'll each tell ten more and now we are up to sixty thousand."

This concept is even better explained by a modern day parable. A priest had a woman come to him to confess gossip. The priest explained that, with sorrow for the sin and a little penance, all would be well. He instructed her to go home and get a feather pillow. The woman objected, asking why she had to do something so silly. Father was insistent. "If you want forgiveness for your sin of gossip, do what I tell you." The woman went home and returned with the pillow a short while later. The priest then instructed her to take the pillow and the pair of scissors which he handed her and go to the upper floor of the church. "Once there," he said, "I want you to open the window, cut open the pillow and shake all of the feathers out of the window."

"Father!" she exclaimed, but the priest insisted she carry out his request. Reluctantly, the woman traveled upstairs to the window the priest mentioned. There, she opened the window, cut open the pillow and shook all the feathers outside. The wind picked up the feathers and, in a moment, they were all over town. The woman returned to the lower floor and explained to the priest her penance was over. She had finished the job. The priest explained that she had only just begun. To finish her penance, he then directed the woman to go outside and pick up all of the feathers. She gasped and said that it would be impossible to pick them all up. The priest said, "The same is true for your gossip. It is impossible to repair the damage once it has been inflicted. Go and sin no more."

After this breakdown story circulated, there were many doors closed to me. This untrue statement forced me out of speaking in the Pittsburgh area for a time and into other parts of the country where my reputation had not been affected. God had His plan. He takes bad and turns it into good. You must be very alert to the way God works. You have to keep your ear to the ground, your eyes wide open, and watch Him all the time. This stuff is super! And people want to go to some evil place like Disneyland or Disney World for fun. Ha! Why would I want to support their large practicing homosexual staff, and their evil movie studios which produce junk like *Priest* and *Kids*, when I can have fun with God?

Some of the attacks become enjoyable. It's fun to watch how Satan tries to manipulate people and events and how God defeats him. When Satan attacks you, don't get so frightened. Just knuckle down and start praying your heart out. Learn how to rebuke him, saying with force, "I command you in the name of Jesus Christ to get out of here!" If you don't rebuke him, he gets his foot in the door. Once his foot is on the threshold, then his arm is inside. Soon it is hard to get him out. Always shut Satan down the instant he arrives.

Don't get upset when people say nasty things about you. People lie. That's no revelation because we are all liars at times. We all have a hard time telling the truth. You will make mistakes and some days Satan will defeat you, just as he defeats me. Believe me, I have gotten angry with people who have stolen from me, lied to me and deceived me. Thank God for priests!

The day the Columbus store closed

I received a call from a group of people in Columbus, Ohio, one day in 1995, asking if I would allow them to participate in Gospa Missions' apostolate by operating a religious store for us in their area. In view of the pressure that was already on all of us at the Mission from being overworked, I was hesitant to allow someone to open another religious gift and book store, especially one so far away. We didn't really have our own act together, let alone be able to support and guide someone else wanting to do the same thing.

But I always try to catch myself before I say no because it is far too easy to say no to God. I reminded myself that I had given too many of those to the Lord already. I'm now in the business of giving yeses to Him. After asking the eager callers a long list of questions in an attempt to ascertain the depth of the desire and their level of commitment, I swallowed hard and said yes to the Columbus group.

When the word got around the Mission about my starting yet another project, I thought some people were going to kill me. Everyone was already working very hard to fulfill all of the commitments I had made.

Satan did not want this store to come on line. The volunteers from Columbus who were to staff the store made several trips to our headquarters in Evans City, Pennsylvania, to transport all of the religious goods from our warehouse to stock the shelves, for it was part of our agreement, since the store was a part of our apostolate, that we would provide all the product to sell.

On one of their stock transfer trips, two people from Gospa Missions verbally attacked the visitors from Columbus. Our office manager at the time was venting frustrations that were caused by this agreement I had made. Then our business manager jumped in and one of the two told the Columbus volunteers that they were going to ruin Gospa Missions. They were told we could not handle the additional work and that they were taking advantage of me. I was on the road evangelizing at the time. When I returned home, I was informed about the confrontation. I immediately got on the telephone and tried to repair the damage with an apology to the Columbus people. It worked to a point, but the ruffling of feathers left some residual animosity.

The two representatives of Gospa Missions who started the confrontation are no longer with us, but the result of their actions then and at other times, will be with us forever. In spite of everything, the store did open about eight weeks later. Now the fruit of the Columbus volunteers' labor was about to unfold. I drove down to Columbus, Ohio for the grand opening celebration. The store looked beautiful.

Satan never took his grip off either side. With his constant badgering and causing many computer problems, he kept everyone at odds. The friction and lack of understanding eventually caused the deterioration of our relationship with the Columbus people.

If you get involved in a project like this and are not rooted in your faith, it will never work. The volunteers at Gospa Missions who caused the problems were not properly rooted in their faith, although they said they came to work for Jesus or the Blessed Mother. The same goes for the Columbus volunteers. To claim you are doing something for God, and then react in a manner contrary to His teachings, brings about failure. The fruit of a good tree is success. In the realm of God, every bad tree is cut down. This tree met with the ax. It was not going to grow in the Gospa garden.

I received a call one day from the volunteer in Columbus who was in charge of the operation. He explained to me that the Columbus store no longer belonged to Gospa Missions. Furthermore, he was going to remove all of the remaining products from their shelves and deliver them to our doorstep. Although this seemed to me to constitute the theft of a store on their part, that's exactly what they did. The Columbus store is now called Gospel Missions and is not affiliated with Gospa Missions at all.

It almost seemed like Satan won. The bad news even came to us on the sixth day of the sixth month of nineteen-ninety-six or 6-6-96. Satan's number in Scripture is 666. To me, that was significant. I had a very large wound in my heart. It is hard to explain how badly something like this hurts. People don't understand the game they are playing. There are not simply stores at stake, but souls.

I guess you are wondering where the miracle is in all of this. The Lord never gives you more than you can handle. Jesus never leaves me lying on the ground for long. The very next day I got a call from Angie Fiello, a very dear friend from the Chicago area. She announced to me that a man whom she knew very well was willing to donate one hundred and twenty-five thousand dollars to Gospa Missions for start-up costs and operating capital for a religious goods store and Gospa Center, which she would operate. What are the odds of that?

A new tree was planted. Some of my heart was repaired. The personal hurt was gone. The only remaining hurt was the part that dealt with the souls of the people that caused the failure of the Columbus store. If it were sin on their part and went unconfessed, it could cost them much. I pray God will forgive us all.

Soon I had to attend another grand opening. This time it was to open the store called *Amazing Grace* in Highland, Indiana. It was situated in an attractive little strip mall right on a main highway. My wife, Mary, was with me for this festive occasion. I cannot tell you with words how beautiful that store looked when we walked in the door. The tears which began to stream down Mary's face explained how beautiful she thought it was. The people involved in setting up the store were Angie and Tony Fiello and Linarae Mueller, in addition to our benefactor, who prefers to remain anonymous. It was obvious they had worked very hard and had put their hearts into the project.

Satan did not stop the attack. The people from Columbus called Angie and tried to talk her out of cooperating with Gospa Missions. They said many unkind things about us. Angie did not believe them, thank God. Her own experience with us did not bear out their allegations. *Amazing Grace* worked for three years the way the Lord intended the Columbus store to work. Unfortunately, it is now closed, but not for lack of faith and effort on the part of the managers. The traffic and the business was just not enough to sustain it on its own. It was a very sad day for all of us when that store closed, but for very different reasons.

Imitation of Christ

Most of the time I never find out about the miraculous occurrences that happen to people at my presentations. It is probably best that I don't find out. Satan is on the prowl all of the time and would just love to convince me that I am something that I am not. Pride can slip into your subconscious so quickly and it has at times.

I can remember a while back doing something very dangerous and being issued a stern warning. "You could lose your life by doing that," my friend pointed out. Now I can't even recall what I was doing that drew so much attention. But my rather arrogant response was, "Do you actually think God is going to let me die so quickly? Where is He going to get another me? Who, today, is going to travel all over the world trying to get people to turn back to God and do it for free? Everybody wants money. Do you think God is going to let something happen to me that easily?"

Those statements were a big mistake on my part. Satan had the better of me that day. But, in one sense, I was just a little correct. God did not let me flounder in that sin for long. He introduced me to a series of audio

121

tapes, *The Imitation of Christ*, by Thomas a Kempis. I highly recommend the tapes to everyone who thinks they have a close relationship with Jesus.

The tapes explained that there is really nothing we can do for God. God already has everything. I learned that even my feeble attempts at doing for God were, in reality, God still doing for me. Let me explain. It was a sin for me to think God needed me for anything. He can do perfectly well without me. What I thought was an effort on my part to help God out *was God still helping me*. He was showering me with graces so I could work off some of the damage I caused to my soul in my twenty-seven-year sabbatical from the Catholic Church.

The woman with a neck injury

Sometimes God allows me a brief encounter with a person who has received a gift from Him. I think it is just to help me to get over some of the attacks. This was the case in a church near Philadelphia.

The evening was over and all of my work was completed in behalf of the Lord. As Mary and I started to walk out, the last two people in the building struck up a conversation with us. One of them was the custodian of the church and his wife. It was this man who, very casually, mentioned his wife's healing to us.

"My wife was in an automobile accident," he said. "Some nerves in her neck were severed." Then the woman herself came into the conversation and explained how she had suffered a lot of pain for an extended period of time. She explained that some nerves were severed and others damaged and the doctors could do no more for her. She said, "Tonight all that pain left after you prayed over me, Tom." Obviously nothing was wrong with her at that point. She was moving freely and had a smile on her face.

What can we say to something like that? "Thank God" is all any of us can say. Then Mary and I left to journey to the next church. We obviously left with our spirits lifted. But the incident was so odd. Had we not lingered at the church a little longer than we usually do, I don't believe we would have ever known that this healing had taken place.

I didn't know at the time that it was one of the gifts from the Lord to help me over an upcoming attack originating from that trip.

I don't doubt that this woman I just described was healed, or any of the others mentioned in this book, because I personally received a healing in my life. I had rheumatoid arthritis and, in one second, Jesus took it all away. There was no investigation to find out if I had really had the disease and if it had truly been taken away, although my medical records will prove it so. In the realm of the world, no miracle occurred. Nevertheless, to me there was a great miracle.

Spikes in His hands

Today we want to investigate everything and apply scientific principles to it in some misguided and relatively feeble attempt to arrive at a "truth" as defined by us. Therefore all "truth" is totally limited to the capabilities our human brains can muster. The inadequacy of such an approach is never more evident than when dealing with the realm of the divine. How about applying Jesus Christ to science instead of the other way around, to find out if the scientists are dealing with the truth?

Let me ask the scientists a question. Is Jesus Christ truly present in the Eucharist - Body, Blood, Soul, and Divinity? If you can't answer a simple truth like that with a profound **yes**, then how can I believe anything you say. Christ alive in the Eucharist is a basic truth.

Many times the challenges to Christianity from the science professionals are, in reality, attacks by Satan. One example is the altering of the crucifixes. For more than nineteen hundred years, all crucifixes had the spikes in the palm of Christ's hands. Now men and women from the scientific professions have presented a case for changing that. Scientists point out that, according to all known laws of science, Jesus could not have hung by His hands, because the flesh of His hands could never have supported His weight while hanging on the cross. Many churches have bought into that teaching and sculptors have actually moved the spikes to Christ's wrists. Look at the crucifix in your church (if you *have* a crucifix in you church.) Are the spikes where science says they should be, or where Scripture says they were?

*"Thomas, called Datums, one of the Twelve, was not with them when Jesus came. So the other disciples said to him, 'We have seen the Lord.' But he said to them, 'Unless I see **the mark of the nails in His hands** and put my finger into the nail marks and put my hand into His side, I will not believe.'*

Now a week later his disciples were again inside and Thomas was with them. Jesus came, although the doors were locked, and stood in their midst and said, 'Peace be with you.'

*Then He said to Thomas, **'Put your finger here and see My hands**, and bring your hand and put it into My side, and do not be unbelieving, but believe.' Thomas answered and said to Him, 'My Lord and my God!'"*   (John 20: 27)

Maybe God, author of the Scripture, does not know the difference between a hand and a wrist. He only created the body, while the scientists have studied it well. The scientists think they know everything.

*"Bind them at your **wrist** . . ."* (Deu 6:8)

*"Therefore, take these words of mine into your heart and soul. Bind them at your **wrist** as a sign."* (Deu 11:18)

125

*"Suddenly, opposite the lampstand, the fingers of a human **hand** appeared, writing on the plaster of the wall in the king's palace. When the king saw **the wrist and   hand** that wrote."* (Dan 5:5)

*"By him was the **wrist** and **hand** sent, and the writing set down."* (Dan 5:24)

It seems that people in those days *did know* the difference between a wrist and a hand. How uninformed then could the author of the Bible be when He related the story of doubting Thomas? Did the Divine Author get the wrist and hand confused?

Or could someone else be confused? Could Jesus have been tied to the cross as well? It seems logical to think that if you were going to drive a nail into someone's hand, you might want to tie him down first to keep the hand in position. It's just another attempt to bring change, and along with it, doubt and questions. If you throw enough false theology against the wall, some will stick.

Prepare for Satan

Recently, I was speaking in the Chicago area and again my friends, Angie, Tony and Linarae, scheduled presentations in several areas. One of these talks was in Munster, Indiana. As a prerequisite for my being permitted to give a two-hour presentation at Saint Thomas More Church in Munster, the pastor asked that I speak at every Sunday Mass prior to my presentation on Monday. That would mean one Mass on Saturday night and four Masses on Sunday

As Catholics, we are allowed to participate in two Masses each day. I went to the Saturday evening Mass and to the four Sunday Masses to extend a brief invitation to everyone to attend my talk. To pique their interest, I mentioned that when I pray for the sick, at times they get well. I prayed the Rosary between the Masses I attended and during the Masses in which I could not participate. *That Sunday I said forty-five decades of the Rosary.*

After the third Mass and my invitation to everyone to come to my presentation, a young lady approached me and asked if I made "house calls." She said, with tears in her eyes, "Not actually a 'house call,' but would you come to the hospital and pray for my mother? She is dying." Her mother had undergone heart surgery and was in a coma and the doctors could not bring her around. The girl said, "It doesn't look good." I said, with a big smile on my face, "Yes, I make 'house calls,'" and we arranged to meet at the hospital later that day.

On my way to the hospital, my friend, Angie, gave me a beautiful white and silver cross to take with me on my mission of mercy. The cross had a relic of the true cross in it. I was grateful for the loan of the cross. You need all the help you can get when you try to work a miracle in the name of the Lord. Besides, the boy in Utah had *my* cross with the relics in it.

I arrived at the hospital and as I was walking down the hall, the Lord said, in the silence of my heart, *"Go in there with faith."* I replied, "Oh, Jesus, I always go with faith." "No!" He insisted. *"I mean **faith**."* I didn't know what He meant.

I then met with the girl who invited me to come and we proceeded to her mother's room in the intensive care unit. When we arrived at the room, I left the girl just outside because the nurse said that only one person was permitted in the room at a time.

When I walked into the room, suddenly all the alarms on the equipment attached to the girl's mother started sounding. I was a bit taken aback by this, but proceeded to walk over to do the job for which I had come. Lying motionless, the woman looked almost dead. I laid my hand on her head and started to pray. As I did this, the woman started kicking and thrashing. She started making all kinds of guttural sounds and then started to vomit.

A nurse ran into the room and started to yell at me, "Get out of here!" In a very shaken state, I left the room. The girl asked me when I came out, "Did you hurt my mother?" Her father was now there and shouted at me, "What the hell did you do to my wife?" Now I understood what the Lord meant when He said to go in there with **faith**. You could never understand how I felt that moment.

I said very assertively to all concerned, "When was the last time this woman has been to Confession or

Mass?" The answer came from the daughter, "My mother has not been inside a Catholic Church in twenty years." I said, "Your mother is going to be all right. However, I want this whole family to go to see a Catholic priest when your mother gets out of the hospital."

I gave the girl the address where I was staying and the phone number. "Call me if you need anything," I said. A day or two later the girl came to visit to say thank you. She related that the hospital was discharging her mother that day.

Look at the preparation the Lord had me go through to ready myself to do this healing. Bear in mind that if I were going to pray for her on my own, I would have never prepared in such a powerful way. I attended five Masses, said forty-five decades of the Rosary and walked in the hospital room carrying a relic of the true cross.

We must be constantly aware of the teachings of Christ. When the apostles were trying to cast out demons from a possessed boy, the miracle would not work because of their lack of preparation. However, Jesus came and laid His hands on him and the boy was cured. Jesus then turned to the apostles and rebuked them, charging them with having little faith. He explained to them that this kind [of healing] takes much prayer. If you look in the footnotes of that Scripture, you will find the words "much fasting."

Jesus Christ always prepared Himself to work miracles. Look what He did before He met Satan in the desert; He fasted for forty days. Many people take the work of the Lord in a frivolous way, as I do at times. Nevertheless, the Lord's teaching is constant, and if you live His way, the joy that you will know becomes your strength.

Bishop Sheen

Even some priests and bishops don't take God seriously at times and some not at all. But I've noticed that the ones who put the Word of God into practice see the miraculous results. They find out that God does notice our efforts and they are great examples for you and me.

All of the training we need to get the important tasks accomplished is in Scripture and the Tradition that was handed down to us. Through some truly fascinating reading, there are valuable lessons to be learned through the lives of our saints. Prayer, fasting, faith and most of all, a willingness to go and do the work of the Lord, are what will make us saints someday. It is so easy to say . . ." I don't have time." That is called working for Satan by default.

I remember a story told by the great evangelist Bishop Fulton J. Sheen. He was asked to go to a hospital, by someone whom he did not even know, to visit this person's dying friend. As busy as he was, Bishop Sheen agreed to go. What a superb example for all bishops and the rest of us.

The bishop went to the hospital and, upon entering the man's room, found that he was not welcome. The man started yelling, "Get out of here! I told everyone I didn't want any priests coming around." Who throws a priest out, but the deceiver? Satan tried to climb all over this bishop. Now let's learn, by reading the following, the right way to handle Satan.

The bishop said, "I come to only visit." The man repeated, "Get out!" Bishop Sheen left. He came back the next day and tried again. Day after day, without fail, Bishop Sheen persisted in trying to win the man over. Each time, the bishop was rejected.

Finally, after fifteen or twenty consecutive days, the man allowed the bishop to stay. This permission was granted under the condition that they would not talk about God. The man hated God. The bishop agreed. They talked about his family and all sorts of things, but not God.

A week or so later it became apparent that the man was now very close to death. Bishop Sheen made another attempt to get the man to go to Confession and receive the sacraments. The man grew very angry and demanded that the bishop leave. Bishop Sheen had now racked up about forty-five consecutive daily visits. The bishop pleaded with him before leaving. "I will go," the bishop said, "but please hear me out. I am leaving my telephone number. If, during the night, you feel the end is near and you want to talk to me, please call. If you become too weak to call, have a nurse do it for you. And as a final resort, when all else fails and you want the Lord to help, just say 'Jesus, have mercy.' May God bless you." The bishop left.

Bishop Sheen returned the next day to find the man's bed empty. He asked the nurse about him and she replied, "He died." "Did he ask for me during the night?" "No," the nurse said. "Did he say anything at all before his death?" he asked the nurse. "Yes, he kept repeating, 'Jesus, have mercy. Jesus have mercy,'" she revealed.

All of this effort came from a bishop with probably more time constraints than most everyone else in the world. Bishop Sheen has to be a saint for just that one act of persistent mercy for one soul. Have you done the same for another human being?

It is when we believe like children that the impossible is accomplished. Bishop Sheen, with all of his intellect, still believed as a child. He met Satan face to face and then defeated him there on the battlefield of life.

That is exactly what Jesus did with me and the woman at the hospital. He prepared me to meet Satan face to face. With Christ at my side, armed with faith, fasting, prayer, and fueled on daily Eucharist, Satan was defeated that day, on that battlefield.

Satan can and will be defeated. Remember that it is a meek, humble, kind, and loving Mother who is going to crush his head. In the meantime, defeat Satan in your life today. You can do it no matter if you're a bishop or a parishioner. Go out as Bishop Sheen did and defeat Satan in the lives of others. Be persistent. Be like this great bishop. Be like your loving Mother.

Thomas Rutkoski

Chapter Eight

God Who Repays Sevenfold

Arizona rainbows

Mary, myself, Joan Ulicny (author of *A Greater Vision*) and others were scheduled to speak at a Gospa Missions outdoor day of Mass, prayer and speakers, which we called *Retreat in the Desert*. The retreat took place between Phoenix and Tucson, Arizona. Also speaking that day were Estella and Reyes Ruiz. They and their family are from Phoenix. This is one of the holiest families I know. They also believe they are experiencing wonderful gifts from the Lord and Blessed Mother. The music for this retreat was provided by James Milanesa, who flew with his mother from California to be with us. The whole day was arranged by Robert Negrette and James Kern, our key men in Tucson.

Robert and James worked hard to publicize the event and get the word out. However, how many people today want to sit out in the torrid Arizona desert sun and listen to stories about how God saves His people?

It was **hot, hot, hot!** About sixty people were all that came to spend the day with God. Everyone in attendance was suffering in some way; some more than others.

Take Reyes Ruiz , for instance. Reyes had been diagnosed with prostate cancer and was suffering badly even without the added burden of the intense heat. He had to come to the retreat lying down in the back of a station wagon. He was not willing to let his suffering stop his evangelization. When it was his turn to speak, his family brought him from the wagon and pushed him in a wheel chair to sit in front of the stage. He and his wife, Estella, had a double impact on everyone's heart that day, first through their spoken message, and second through Reyes's drive to serve the Lord. A perfect example of practicing in real life, the prayer, *"Here I am, Lord. I have come to do Your will."*

It was a typical Gospa Missions Retreat. What made this retreat typical was the miracle that occurred. You see, miracles usually occur at the retreats we sponsor.

On this particular day, after the Mass, many people were drawn to look to the sky. Lo and behold, in a perfectly clear blue sky, appeared four completely horizontal rainbows stacked one on top of the other.

I have seen two rainbows in the sky at one time before, but never four. And certainly not in a clear sky. Rainbows always occur when it is stormy, with the sun peeking through the rain-filled sky. That is what causes a rainbow - the light refracts through the raindrops to give us the full spectrum of colors.

Also, all rainbows I've ever seen have been shaped like, well, rainbows! They have an arch to them. Maybe that is where the "bow" part of the word comes from. However, these rainbows were not arched, but formed four straight lines. And they still had all the colors of the spectrum. Guess who we thought sent it?

There is not going to be any investigation to see if any of these miracles, as I call them, are truly miracles. If any of them were submitted to a bishop for evaluation, the result would most assuredly be that nothing supernatural had occurred. So God doesn't inspire people very often to go running to the official Church shouting, "It's a miracle, it's a miracle." You have to take them into your heart and know that God did it just for you and not the whole world. Scripture tells us how the Blessed Mother took all of the Christ-incidences in her life into her heart.

God just touches one heart here and one there, then goes about His business of saving the ones that "believe as children." Children, children, children . . . become like children. Do not become like theologians or investigators or scientists or even those who rewrite God's already perfect Word.

We were like children that day in the Arizona desert, oohing and aahing at the marvel in the sky. It was as though Our Father was saying, "Thank you for wanting to spend a day with Me in the desert. Thank you for suffering just a little for Me."

A boy's foot is healed

At the same retreat, a woman from Tucson brought her son over to me to say thank you. I asked them why they were thanking me. She answered, "You came to speak in Tucson and my son and I heard that sometimes people with physical problems were helped by the Lord through you. We came to your presentation and enjoyed hearing all that God has done for you, and how He came and saved you when no Catholics would. After your presentation, you prayed over the whole crowd, one at a time. I brought my son up and he received from you the Blessed Mother's blessing. We were praying for help from the Lord because my son, at the time, had a club foot. It was very difficult for him to walk. Well, you can see for yourself, the problem is ninety percent corrected. It didn't happen right at the moment you prayed for him, but we noticed the next day he was walking well."

I think the Lord was listening when I asked Him to wait until I get out of town before He works His miracle so I won't get blamed for it. But often I come back to a town and hear of the great gifts the Lord gave to people after I left. I like it that way. It takes the focus off me and puts it where it belongs. I must admit, though, I do need the positive reinforcement from time to time.

Hearing about these gifts helps me to keep going. Still today, the very Catholics who should have come for me while I was away from my faith for twenty-seven years continue to pour cold water on my conversion. Even the religious try to steal what God is doing for me, and for others through me.

The boy's mother said to me, "My son wants to ask you a question. May he do that?" "Of course," I responded. I turned to the lad and said, "What is it, son?" He looked up at me with such trust in his eyes and asked, "Will you ask God to fix my foot the rest of the way?" A big smile came on my face and I said, "Why do you want Him to do that?" He answered, "Because the other kids make fun of me when I can't do all the things they can do and because I still walk a little funny."

I said to the boy, "Walk over to that table and back for me." He did what I asked, and when he returned, I said, "You walk just fine. Things are not always perfect in this world and sometimes it's because that is the way God wants it. Do you see these two fingers on my left hand? They are not very pretty, are they? When I was your age, I had a blasting cap blow up in my hand. Blasting caps are like big firecrackers. The explosion took off the tip of my index finger and the top of my thumb. After I got out of the hospital and the bandages were removed, I could see how badly my fingers looked. You would think people would be sympathetic and feel bad for me, but people are people, and so they made fun of me. It really hurt my feelings back then when I was young. Now I can see that this terrible accident actually helped make me a stronger person. It most certainly gave me the opportunity to learn to forgive.

God blessed you in a big way, and He must have left this little problem with your foot to give you an opportunity to forgive when the kids make fun of you. Nobody is perfect. Go and be happy with what God has already done for you." He walked away happy and with a new understanding. The boy was growing up.

That is true for all of us. We want to be perfect so that when people look at us they will be impressed at how beautiful or handsome we are. We worry about how well we are dressed, how we smell, and what our hair looks like. Oh, if we only were so concerned about our souls and how well-groomed they are.

In the end it doesn't matter how good we looked, what kind of car we drove, or who had a bigger house. It all rots and turns to nothing but dirt, as we will also. Keep in mind, maggots are going to eat our bodies. We can't take anything with us. There will be no U-Haul trailers following the hearse at our funeral.

Satan has us all chasing an illusion. We try to outdo each other in all things and lose sight of the perfection that lasts. God sends gifts, like the day in the desert and the healing of a young boy's foot, to keep us focused on one goal - Heaven. To get there, we have to constantly strive to be perfect, as our heavenly Father is perfect.

Chapter Nine

Conversion

My dying mother

We again draw from the treasure of grace stored in *Apostles of the Last Days.* This story from my other book needs repeating here because it shows how conversion of the heart each day leads to spiritual growth and the exactness of God in answering prayer. This story is a foundation for the one that follows.

My mother, Anna Rutkoski, contracted cancer in the mid 1970s. She lived with cancer for about ten years. She would be extremely ill and then the doctors would give her some radiation and she would be well for a while. Back and forth, good health, then bad again. Finally, there was no more treatment for my mother. My sisters and I, along with the doctors, put her in a hospice program for the terminally ill. The plan was to make her as comfortable as possible. The whole family agreed that there would be no more radiation, and Mom would live out her days, months or years, whatever God's will might be.

I knew the phone call would come one day, and it did. My sister, Elizabeth, in Tampa, Florida, called and said, "Tom, you better get down here right away. Mom probably won't make it more than a day or two." I hopped on a plane as fast as I could.

The only thing that slowed me down was some trouble I was having with a judge in Erie, Pennsylvania. I was supposed to be a juror at a trial during the very same time that my mother was dying. A call to ask the judge if I could be excused was fruitless. His reply was, "No! Everybody's mother is dying," he said. Then, in a nasty way, he barked, "If you don't show up, I will hold you in contempt of court!"

Talk about contempt. Some judges in the United States have gone mad. No prayer in schools, but it is okay to kill the children in your womb. And you can't be with your dying mother because of jury duty. Many judges are in contempt of God!

I called my attorney and asked what to do. He said he would call the judge and have this all worked out for me. The call from my attorney upset the judge to the point that he called me and reiterated that if he had any more contact from anyone about me and my problem, he would hold me in contempt of court. That statement is a perfect example how people act when they don't have God in their lives.

Yes, I was leaving without permission from the judge. He finally, just before departure, sent a message that I could go, but I was already on my way. On the way down to Tampa, I said a simple prayer, "Jesus, could I spend one good week with my mother before you take her? That's all I ask. One good week."

I arrived in Tampa and proceeded to my sister's house. She took me directly to the room where my mother was lying in bed. My mother had not been out of bed in months. I walked into that room with a fake smile on my face and some false enthusiasm. I did not want my mother to see her death on my face. I said, "Hi, Mom, how are you doing? It is your son Tommy. Come on, get up out of that bed and we'll have a glass of wine and we'll talk about what we are going to do the rest of the week. We are going out shopping, out to dinner, and we'll go visit your friends. Come on get up and out of that bed!" My mother rolled around ever so slowly. I could see her agonizing just to move. She looked over at me, and in the weakest little voice she managed to say, "Okay, son, I'll try." My eyes welled with tears instantly. I couldn't take it. My mother looked so weak. I said, "I've got to go, Mom." I ran out of the room. Seeing how sick my mother really was broke my heart.

I left Mom's bedroom and went to the living room to visit with my sister, Elizabeth (her nickname was Betts). We talked for about fifteen minutes when, all of a sudden, as she stared behind me, my sister's eyes grew very large. I said, "What's the matter, Betts?" She said, "Your mother is up!" I turned around and found my mother standing there. In a little stronger voice than before she said, "I think I'll have that wine now." So we had a glass of wine and talked a little bit. About fifteen minutes later she said, "Well, I'd better go back to bed and get my rest if we are going to go do all those things the rest of the week." It made me shake my head in wonder. My sister also couldn't believe what had just happened.

My mom went back to bed and soon my sister and I turned in for the night. I got up about 7:30 in the morning, took my shower, and got dressed. I went into the living room and to my amazement, there was my mother sitting there, fully dressed. She looked twenty years younger. She said in a voice only a well mother can use on her son, "What took you so long? You said you were taking me out to breakfast today and then shopping. You said we could go see my friends."

There was nothing wrong with my mother! In fact, the whole week there was nothing wrong with my mother. We did go to visit her friends - the very friends who had been coming to see her on her deathbed. We went out to dinner and to the shopping mall. She was amazed at the people in the walkers and wheelchairs and then she said, "Look at that! I was like that not too long ago and look at me now!" Oddly enough, the miracle that was happening was not sinking into my sister's head. She was actually *upset* over the whole situation. She called my wife back in Pennsylvania, and said, "You know that husband of yours, with all his God business? If you think you had a problem with him before, wait until he comes home. Now he thinks he's a faith healer!"

The hospice program phoned in the middle of the week. They said to my sister, "We will be out to your house around 3:00 p.m. today to wash Mrs. Rutkoski."

My sister said, "Don't bother." They said, "Oh, she died?" Betts said, "No, she's out at the shopping mall with my brother!" Betts was still upset about the whole scenario. She just could not understand.

At the end of the week my mom said, "Son, can I come home with you?" "Sure, Mom, absolutely," was my reply. My sister pulled me aside and said, "What is going on here?" I told Betts, "Your mother is coming home to die."

My mother flew home and no sooner had she arrived when she said, "Son, I don't feel so well right now. Can I lie down a little bit?" Mother said the trip probably wore her out. She lay down to rest that day, but soon afterwards she began to decline quickly. In a couple of weeks, she passed away.

This is a fantastic God we have here. A simple prayer backed up with daily Mass, fifteen decades of the Rosary, and fasting on bread and water on Wednesdays and Fridays brings all of this about. I asked, "Lord, may I spend one good week with my mother before You take her?" He gave me seven perfect days. If you take God seriously, prayer works.

Mary Jane goes to dinner

In retrospect, I see how my prayer for my mother was actually a lack of faith. Let me explain.

Both my sisters, Betts and Mary Jane, live in Tampa. In the spring of 1994, I got a call from that same sister, Betts. She said, "Tom, you better get down here right away. Mary Jane just had a massive brain hemorrhage and may not live." "Betts, I can't come down. I have to speak in Canton tomorrow night and then the next day in Akron" and the list went on and on. She retorted, "You mean you would actually do that God stuff rather than coming down here and being with your dying sister?" I replied, "Yes, that is exactly what I mean."

You see, I think differently now. When you really take God seriously, you are involved in the conversion process. Conversion is an everyday affair. It does not happen one time and then it's over. God had now converted me to the point of putting Him before me and my family. Yes, I think quite a bit differently now.

What good would it do for me to go running down to Florida to be at my sister's bedside? To do what, pray? I can pray at home. To encourage her? She had a brain hemorrhage; she was unconscious. What good was I going to accomplish in Tampa? It was better for me to go out to do my talks. If God sees me busy at His work, what is He going to do? Is He going to chastise me for that? No, He is going to reward me! If you busy yourself with God's work, He will go so far out in front of you and take care of your problems that when you look at what He did for you, you will be astounded.

You can just forget about your problems. Scripture says not to worry about tomorrow, today has enough problems of its own. Will all of your problems go away? Not always, and maybe even tougher problems will come. If you implement what God is teaching you *here,* you will find that some problems will go away because you went into the vineyard and worked rather than having paid attention to them. After that, the tougher tests come to see if you have grown some. Tests come over and over again. We always complain when we get tests from God. Did you attend college? The people who did know how many times they had to stay up all night, cramming for tests. For everything we do *well* in life, we have to put out an effort. Where is the effort for God?

My effort for my sick sister was going to be out in the vineyard, not at her bedside. I stayed away for about three weeks. After that, I had a few free days, so I flew down to Florida and went to visit Mary Jane.

Mary Jane had deteriorated into a "worst case" scenario. The doctors said if she didn't come out of the anesthesia after the operation and spring back quickly, she would probably be a vegetable the rest of her life. Mary Jane stayed in a coma for weeks.

When I finally arrived at the hospital, Mary Jane was just starting to come out of her coma. I walked over to her and I said, "Come on, Mary Jane, get up out of that bed. We are going for a ride." She rolled over, smiled and now she was speaking. She said in a very slurred voice, "It's nice to see you. Where is Mary?" I said, "Mary didn't come. She doesn't like you." Betts was standing there and she slapped me on the shoulder saying, "What's wrong with you? Why would you say something like that to your sister?" In response I said, "You know something else, Mary Jane? Your sister Betts doesn't like you either! Now get up and get out of that bed!" She started to laugh and then she said, "Oh, you are always so funny." She sat up.

I said, "Come on, let's get a wheelchair over here and we'll go for a little ride." I had a bit of trouble with the nurse. She believed it was too soon for Mary Jane to get up. I told her to ask the doctor. The end result was that we were going for a ride. I got her out of bed, put her in the wheelchair and I wheeled her outside. God provided some props in a squirrel and some seagulls. I went to the candy machine and got some nuts and we started feeding them. Life started to come back to Mary Jane very quickly. She really brightened up out there.

I took her back to the room and the nurses were shocked at the difference. I told the nurse, "Do whatever you have to do, because tomorrow I'm taking my sister out to a restaurant for dinner." The nurse said, "Mr. Rutkoski, you can't do that. Your sister is very ill!" I said, "You don't understand. She will be fine. I am the custodian. I can check her out of the hospital now if I want to. Go see the doctor." Immediately she ran to the doctor to check this out and the doctor said, "The man is right; he can check her out of the hospital today if he chooses."

I rolled back the curtain in Mary Jane's room and pointed outside. I said to her, "Do you see that sign for the restaurant on that mall over there? Well, I am taking you over there tomorrow and we are going out to dinner." Mary Jane laughed. She thought I was being silly.

The next day the hospital staff insisted that Mary Jane partake in some rehabilitation to practice getting in and out of a car. She did it two or three times and finally I said, "Come on, let's go! You know how to get into a car."

We went outside and I brought the car to the door. It wasn't like Mary Jane jumped into the car. She had some difficulty, but she did it. Off we went. What a good time she was having. I tried to joke about things a lot, more than normal, to keep Mary Jane's spirits up. We drove around a bay and crossed a bridge and there it was - the beautiful mall that I pointed out to her from her bedside.

I parked the car and Mary Jane was able to walk from the car to the mall. She was a little slow in her gait, but returning ever closer to normal. She was astounded that we were actually doing this. We were walking down the corridor of the mall toward the restaurant where I wanted to take her. The restaurant was at the opposite end of the mall, so it took a while to get there.

My sister's ability to walk increased as we covered the length of the building. Even as we talked, her speech was noticeably improving. By the time we arrived at the end of the corridor, she was walking perfectly well and speaking normally. There was a woman's shop on the left, just before the entrance to the restaurant that I had chosen. My sister said, "Do you mind if I stop in here and shop a little bit? I would like to get a new blouse so I will look nice when I check out of the hospital." When you have a woman who has just gone through brain surgery and who now wants to go shopping, you have a healing! She went in and bought herself a blouse. We then went and had a marvelous dinner. What an appetite. The only thing I wouldn't let her have was the glass of wine that she wanted. When we finished, I took her back to the hospital and again they could not believe the difference.

I had to leave after my three-day visit, but the doctor's prognosis for my sister and reality were two very different things. Mary Jane, who was supposed to be a vegetable for the rest of her life, left the hospital a few days later. She looked, talked and acted almost as well as she did before. It was a miracle.

I begged Mary Jane to understand what a gift God had given to her. I begged her to change the kind of life she was living and to correct her problem of being away from the Church.

Maybe you, the reader, can say a prayer for her? Maybe all of our prayers combined will pour upon her and she will come back to the Church and take God seriously. This is her second chance to live her life the Lord's way. None of us ever knows when God will turn off the flow of grace. And just as when I received my second chance at life, I could have said yes or no. We all get to choose. God forces no one.

Maybe with your prayers, we can bring her spiritual healing to fruition. A miracle on the body is only a manifestation of Divine Power. Saving a soul is the work of Jesus Christ. He is after her soul. God made her well to get her attention. This miracle did not do it this time. She believes she has a good relationship with God, but she is deceived. She thinks she does not have to go to church, but that she can make her own rules. That is precisely why we have 27,000 different denominations of Christianity. People think they can make their own rules and they cannot! I need your help. Please pray for my sister. We will work the second half of this miracle together.

While you are at it, please pray for my sister Betts, also. She, too, is away from her Catholic faith. Same scenario - she thinks all she has to do is tell God that she loves Him and all is well. I won't go into all the reasons she won't go through the process of becoming Catholic again. If you will help me pray for her, she will come home, too.

Thomas Rutkoski

Chapter Ten

Discernment

A three-night dream

This next series of miracles is probably more of a daylong discussion than a chapter in a book. I am going to try to keep it short. The story is a prime example of discernment, something that is badly lacking in the Church today, especially among the laity. Many people are hearing voices, just as I did, but there are two voices out there. One of those voices caused a third of the angels to be evicted from Heaven.

It all started with a dream. Not one of your standard, regular nighttime dreams. This was real-life drama. (By the way, this is not the story which caused the priest I mentioned earlier to think I'd had a nervous breakdown, although I can understand how this could cause people to wonder about me.) Throughout this entire episode, I wanted no part of any of it, but I never want to say no to God again. I agonized over every detail of what is about to unfold.

This dream lasted three nights. Each night I would have this dream and it would end when I awoke in the morning. The next night, when I would go to sleep, it would continue exactly where it left off. I would wake

153

up in the morning and the dream would stop. Then again, the next night, it picked up right where it left off. It was astounding! It was like a three-part mini-series.

It all began with me standing on the back porch of my house looking across the fields of my small farm, which is a little less than thirty acres. I was looking at a valley, or rather where a valley used to be. The valley, in my dream, is turned into a flat piece of land. The reason it became flat is that I had just built a large underground building there and covered it over with soil and planted crops on top of it. You couldn't even tell that it was there. I had my arms folded across my chest, and I was just extraordinarily proud that I had accomplished this enormous project. Then the Lord spoke to me and said, *"Thomas, that isn't where I wanted that building."*

"What are you talking about, Lord?" I asked in amazement. "Do you know how much work it took to build this building?"

He stated, *"I want the building over by the Stations of the Cross."* The Lord was referring to the five acres of woods on my farm in which I had erected the Stations of the Cross. They were a quarter mile to the southeast of where I had placed the building in the first part of my dream. Now the Lord is telling me that He wanted the building over there!

God ignored my objections and continued on with the dimensions of the building. He stated, "I want the building to be sixty feet long, I want it to be forty-four feet wide. I want the interior height to be ten feet. I want the walls to be one foot thick, of poured concrete. I want the ceilings to be two feet thick and the whole structure to be steel-reinforced. I want the drainage to be done in this way," and so on. He went on to lay out for me all the details of this building. On the third day, when this dream was apparently over, I then asked, "God, are you trying to tell me that you actually want this building to be built?" I even exclaimed, "I don't believe this is You, Lord. This is crazy! Look, if this is really You, it would take so much confirmation to get me to do this, that it would be mind-boggling!"

This guy was more than a little bit inquisitive and not totally believing. Walking back to look at the site, the dream started again. It started with me standing there in broad daylight. I was oblivious to everything around me. I could see people working my farm. I did not know any of them. They were using all hand tools. This seemed unusual to me because I own a tractor and other farm equipment and cannot imagine working the soil by hand.

Later, back at the house, I called a man I had just met. This man had told me that he was some kind of contractor - I could not remember what kind. I called him, told him who I was and said, "Hey, Regis, you said you were a contractor?" He answered in the affirmative. I said, "Let me bounce something off you. There is a building I have questions about . . ." and I started giving him the design of my "dream building" and how it was laid out. I asked, "Is this building practical? Does it make sense? Is it sound thinking?" I figured if I could determine that the design and specifications of this structure were faulty, then I would know for certain that all of this was not from God. God doesn't make design or engineering errors. Intrigued, he asked, "Where are you putting it?"

Instantly, I answered, "I never said I was putting it anywhere." I didn't want to be blamed for this thing! Regis retorted, "Oh, come on! You can tell me." I countered, "I just want to hear what you have to say. Is it sound thinking?" To my complete astonishment he said, "I'll be right out." He lives about fifty miles from me, but he was at my farm in about an hour and a half and began unloading survey equipment.

"Come on, where are you putting it?" he coaxed. I replied, "Regis, I could get in trouble for even talking about something like this!" He reassuringly answered, "I won't tell anybody." I relented and took him to the spot where the building was supposedly to be built. He removed from his truck some equipment and started to survey the property.

Three days later there were some basic blueprints for this building at my door. If I wanted to build something of much lesser magnitude and I needed blueprints for it, I can guarantee that I would not see them in three days. How could this happen that I make one speculative phone call and I find someone who does the blue-prints that quickly, without my even asking?

The next day my phone rang. It is a woman who said her name was Sister Louis Marie de Montfort. She said, "Mr. Rutkoski, what is it that you want from me?" I said, "Excuse me, I don't even know you!" She said, "Your name keeps coming into my life and I want to know why." I asked, "What do you mean? How is my name coming into your life?" Sister said, "I was going to Bosnia and about five different people said, " If you are going to Bosnia, call Tom Rutkoski. He goes there a lot." Or she would hear, "Go with Tom Rutkoski. Don't go with any-body else." She said to me that person after person kept saying that. She told them, "I don't need this Rutkoski guy. I already have my trip set up. I am going by my-self." She was getting tired of hearing the name.

Sister Louis Marie eventually went to Bosnia on her own and found herself staying in the same house tin which I always stay when I visit there. What are the odds of that? She found a book laying on the table in this house. The title, *Apostles of the Last Days,* was in-teresting enough to cause her to pick up the book. Sister was flabbergasted to find out it was written by Thomas Rutkoski! She then related that she started to read the book, but she couldn't finish it before she had to leave for home. It was not her book, so she left it behind. To her great surprise, when she arrived home, she found my book was in her mailbox and she had not ordered it.

Sister Louis then told me that she had attempted to discuss with one of her friends, a problem she was having. The person told her that she should call Tom Rutkoski for the answer. For Sister Louis Marie, that had been the last straw. So she had called and now said to me, "Here I am. What do you want?"

Slightly amused by her story, I said to her, "I don't know what is going on, Sister. Look, I speak all over the world. Maybe you are supposed to set up some talks." She said, "I can do that. I'll set some up on Long Island for you. But if I do this for you, how about you do something for me?"

"What's that, Sister?" I asked. She said, "I am looking for a place to put a new holy order. How about helping me search for the right place?" "Oh, my goodness," I exclaimed. "I have been praying for three months for a holy order to come forward. There is a group of us trying to save a shrine called The Most Holy Name of Mary, in Donora, Pennsylvania. I am looking for a holy order to present to the diocese, so that maybe we can save this place. It is about to be closed." She said, "I'll be right out." Sister hopped on a plane and came to Evans City.

When sister arrived, we went to see Bishop Donald Wuerl. Successfully arranging a meeting on such short notice with any bishop is a small miracle in itself. At the meeting, we discussed the possibility of purchasing the

Donora shrine. The bishop was not opposed to the idea, but he informed us that this wasn't a good time for such a project. He had many problems in the diocese and had to solve them first.

After our meeting with Bishop Wuerl, I took Sister Louis Marie out to the farm. I said, "Look, Sister, after all that has happened in our lives, what we should do is thank God and the Blessed Mother. Let's go down and pray the Stations of the Cross. We went down to that piece of woods where I had built my little holy spot and we prayed the Stations.

After we completed the Stations of the Cross I said, "Sister, can I bounce something off you? Something is happening in my life and I can't talk to anybody about it because it's, well, *unusual,* to say the least. If I start talking about this, people are going to think I am crazy!" She asked, "Like what?" I continued, "You see this little valley right here? I had a dream that lasted three nights. In that dream, the Lord was asking me to build some kind of building here . . . underground."

She exclaimed, "Oh, my goodness! That's the same dream that Father Stephen Valenta had. He just doesn't know where the farm is. Let's go call him!" I said, "What? Who is Father Stephen Valenta?" She said, "You don't know Father Stephen Valenta? He is the 'Pray with the Heart' priest! He prays and speaks all over the world. Come on! Let's go call him!"

I could not remember ever hearing of a Father Valenta. We ran up to my house and Sister Louis Marie then called this priest. When he answered, I heard Sister say to him, "Father, you know that dream you had about the underground building? I found the farm where it is to be built!" She insisted, "You've got to come here! The man who owns the land is having some kind of event the first weekend in June. Come out here for that event."

(I couldn't hear the other half of this phone conversation but afterwards, Sister Louis Marie related to me the gist of his side of the dialogue.) Father said, "Let me check my calendar; I think I am booked up then." He looked up the date on his calendar and came back to the phone and said, "No, I can't come. I am speaking somewhere that weekend." She said, "Well, where are you going? Maybe you can just pass through the area and stop by." He said, "Well, it is somewhere in Pennsylvania." She exclaimed, "This is in Pennsylvania!" He replied, " My talk is in a little town called Evans City, Pennsylvania."

Sister turned and said to me, "Are you pulling my leg?" I questioned, "Why, Sister? I can't hear the other end of the conversation. What is he saying?" She excitedly said, "This priest is coming to your event!" I answered, "I don't know anything about that. Somebody sent us a little clip of paper that talked about praying with the heart. That's what the Blessed Mother tells us to do, so I told my staff to invite this priest, not really knowing who he was or what he was about." She said, "That's Father Stephen Valenta!"

Father did not wait for the scheduled event to come to Evans City. He came in a short time later. He called me from a local car dealership and told me he was in the area. Could I come and meet him? I went and picked him up and brought him to my house.

My wife, Mary, was sitting in the kitchen, doing paperwork, when Father and I came in. She was kind of distraught. There were several volunteer workers up in the guest bedroom which I had turned into an office. At that time, I was operating Gospa Missions out of our house. This did not make Mary very happy. She believed all of those people upstairs, and now another coming in the door, were invading her private space. This actually had concerned her for months, and at that particular moment, Father must have been able to see that in her face. Her chagrin was most certainly evident in her demeanor. I introduced Father to her. Father, in his bubbly way, said, "Hi, Mary, it is nice to meet you." Mary, in a very cantankerous manner, looked up and acknowledged Father's presence, but barely. We were out of there fast.

Father ventured upstairs with me and he could see everybody happily at work. He pulled me aside after a while and said, "Thomas, you have violated the sanctity of your home. Gospa Missions has to leave here." I said, "What are you talking about?" He said, "You have got to take this mission and get it out of your house." I retorted, "I can't do that! We don't have any money . . . Gospa Missions is broke!" He chided me, "After what God has been doing in your life . . . you should know better than that!"

I told him that I was actually aware that there was a problem and that I was looking for another place, however, everything was too expensive. He said, "Where did you look?" I said, "There is a little place down in Evans City." He said, "Come on! Let's go look at it." He got me out the door and we drove the three miles to Evans City. I showed him the building. It was unoccupied and for rent. Father said, "Let's go find the owner." Quickly, he found the owner, who happened to be headquartered across the street. The two of them started negotiating while I stood there. The owner wanted fifteen hundred dollars a month. I almost choked. "Fifteen hundred dollars a month!" I exclaimed. Father advised me, "Go get a copy of your book." I did so and Father gave it to the owner of the building with this instruction, "Read this book tonight and call Mr. Rutkoski tomorrow morning and tell him what you will *really* charge him to rent this space."

The man actually read the book that night. He called me in the morning and said, "I would really like to help you out here. The mortgage on the building is a thousand dollars a month. I will let you have it for the mortgage." He came down five hundred dillars. That was thirty-three percent off, a nice discount. I said, "Great negotiating, Father! But I don't have a thousand dollars a month." Father said, "You know better than that! God will provide."

Hopefully I didn't upset the Lord, but I laid down a lot of parameters regarding "His" building. When I saw some of the little confirmations starting to come, I began to insist on big-time confirmation. I said things to Him like, "It will take a lot of money to build this underground building. Where will we get the funds?" I had quit my job for the Lord and I had no personal income. Not only did I not have the funds to build the large building the Lord wanted, now I was now going in debt to the tune of a thousand dollars a month.

Only because of Father Valenta's insistence did we move into the space in Evans City, which had formerly been a clothing store. It had big glass windows in the front. I did not want people looking into the windows and seeing all of the computer equipment that we used in running Gospa Missions. My thought was that, if the computers were plainly visible, someone might try to steal them. I asked some volunteers to help me build a barrier wall to block the view. So we built a partition about fifteen feet back from the windows and covered it with paneling.

We did all our work behind this wall and all was well. We had far more room than we needed, but if this is what God wanted, who am I to question? There was one problem. I had an empty storefront sitting there. I thought that if the townspeople heard that this was a religious mission and looked in the window and saw nothing, they might conclude that it was a front for something illegal. Maybe they would think it was a drug operation or something. What if I made a bad name for the Blessed Mother?

The volunteers had the idea of putting a few statues in the front store area, making it look as though they were for sale. A good idea. So we put a few things out and made it look like a store. People knocked on the door and wanted to buy the products. The merchandise disappeared almost instantly. We put more things out and they sold, too.

There were a few religious stores around. The one closest to us was in Butler, a town of about forty-seven thousand people, about fifteen miles from us. They went bankrupt. There was a religious wholesaler in Lyndora, a town of five thousand people. This operation was even a little bit closer to us, but there was not much demand for wholesale religious goods in that area so they closed their doors as well. Even in Pittsburgh, about thirty miles away, there were religious stores and some of them closed. There did not seem to be enough people buying religious goods these days. Attendance at Mass on Sunday has plummeted to twenty-seven percent of registered Catholics (sound familiar, by now?). That is why all the stores were having a bad time.

We had our little "pretend" store in an old-line, mostly Protestant, farm community of about eight hundred people. That would be the most unlikely place for a Catholic religious store to do any business at all. Right? In the first sixth months, we put a few things out and then some more and we grew and grew until we had to move the wall we built. Then we had to add a second room for the store. Then we needed a warehouse area Then we added a mail order division. In the first six months, we did a half-million dollars worth of business, and netted two hundred and fifty thousand dollars. *It was exactly the estimated cost of the building that God supposedly wanted.* This did not even seem possible, but there was my answer to the first question I had put to Him, "Where am I going to get that kind of money?"

I was very troubled and didn't know what to do. I pleaded, "This is not enough, Lord. I still don't believe this is You. Satan can do stuff like this. You are going to have to send more confirmation.

Okay, if this is You, I will know it when someone donates all of the steel reinforcing rods that we need." I heard in my head instantly, *"Call Crown Wrecking."* No way was I going to call Crown Wrecking! You see, Bobby Crown, the owner, was an old friend from my early KDKA days. I had just told the Lord that I would build the building if He got me the steel rods. If I called Bobby Crown and he donated the rods, I would have to fulfill my part of the bargain. I didn't want to have to do that. It would make me look like a fool. I would not call.

In the meantime, we had escalated our retreats on my farm to two per year. Many people started to come there to pray. We host a day of Mass, Rosary, speakers, confession, music and a healing service. People could go to that little piece of woods and do the Stations of the Cross, also. These retreats are very special and they became very popular. A place of great conversion. At most retreats we experienced people returning to the sacraments who had been away from the Church for ten, twenty, and as many as forty years.

I get so busy sometimes. In the summer of 1993, the volunteers were badgering me because I had not yet scheduled anyone to be the main speaker at our September 4 retreat, and it was about a month away. I had just come back from a lengthy speaking tour and I had many phone calls to return. There was also a ton of mail to be read and answered. I pleaded, "Come on, give me a break. . . . I can't do it all." I told my helpers that I needed a little time to rest. However, that day there was no rest.

I was opening the mail and I started reading a flyer. It contained an article on a woman named Maria Esperanza. She was from Betania, Venezuela in South America. I had never heard of her before. This article claimed that this woman is visited by the Blessed Mother. It further asserted that she had been known to bi-locate, levitate and heal the sick. It went on and on. I said, "Wow! Where does God come up with people like this? This is fantastic!"

One of the guys came into my office with a flyer. He said, "Hey, Tom, look. Here is a flyer on Josyp Terelya. Do you know who he is?" I replied, "Yeah, I know who he is." The volunteer said, "Invite Josyp to the retreat." I remember thinking how ridiculous a suggestion it was - to invite someone as well-known and in demand as Josyp Terelya with only a three-week notice. Like he was going to come. I held up the flyer I had been reading and I said, "Yeah, and why don't I invite Maria Esperanza?" Then that voice in my head said, *Yes, invite Maria Esperanza.*

I looked on the flyer and there was a number for a Father Heffernan in Peterborough, Ontario, Canada, and I dialed the number. The priest answered the phone. I said, "Father, I was reading a flyer about a woman named Maria Esperanza. Do you know her?" He answered, "Yes, I know her." I explained, "We are having a retreat in Pennsylvania in September and I would like to invite her to come here." He said, "When? Next year?" I answered, "No, in three weeks." He questioned, "Do you know whom you are talking about?" I thought, "She bi-locates, she levitates, heals the sick, is visited by the Blessed Mother and is approved by the Church. It sounds good to me."

Father explained, "She is one of the most sought-after visionaries on the face of the earth! What makes you think she is going to drop everything and come to your farm in a couple of weeks?" Apparently believing he had spoken too hastily, he then said, "Look, I'm sorry. I am not going to be the no in your life. I'll let her do that." So he called down to Venezuela and told Maria Esperanza about my request. She was so enthralled that anyone would have the nerve to even ask her to travel so far on such short notice that she wanted to know who this person was. She said, "Have this man write me a letter and fax it to me. I want to hear about this. Have him explain why I should drop everything in my life and come running to a country I have never been to before and with only three weeks notice."

I wrote her a letter that went something like this:

Dear Mrs. Esperanza,

For twenty-seven years I had given God all nos in my life. In His infinite mercy, He came and saved my soul anyhow. I am so overwhelmed by that kind of mercy that I have given my life to Him. Now, not only do I try to give Him all yesses, I go all over the world trying to get everybody else to give Him yesses.

So I guess what I am trying to do is to get you to say yes. But what difference does it make if I want you to come, or I don't want you come, to this retreat? What matter does it make if you want to come or you don't want to come? What does that have to do with anything? I believe it has more to do with this: does the Mother of God want you to come to this retreat? You say she visits you. The next time she shows up, why don't you ask *her* if she wants you on my farm on September 4th?

In Jesus and Mary,
Thomas Rutkoski

Maria Esperanza wrote back on August 10.

Dear Mr. Tomas,

I appreciate the value of your spirituality and practicality which you radiate in each word, conceiving ideas that conform a beautiful group of painter's strokes and signs of renovation of the life of faith that touches the heart. And this has moved me very much, for I see how in such a simple way you say what you feel. In such manner, this woman responds Yes!, and this yes is because I infinitely love my Mother, and she, Mary, the Mother of Jesus and Our Mother, wants me to follow her in search for her sons and daughters, children, youth, adults, elderly, to gather them all in her Motherly heart. She is so good, soft and generous that she does not know how to tell you anything but, "Yes! my son, yes! Here I am to help you with the burden . . . and give you the breath of hope . . . over your ar-

dent chest . . .desirous to help my little ones
with a beautiful Day, full of Peace and the hap-
piness of the innocent child. May God keep you!"

This is why Mr Tomas that here you have a Yes!
A yes from the Holy Mother, she Mary the
humble maiden of Nazareth, pure and chaste,
and also as the courageous woman of Calvary! . .
Thank you! And may Our Lord keep your steps.

God bless you,
Maria E[speranza] de Bianchini

I thought it might be a little bit cocky on my part to
believe that the Blessed Mother cares about what I am
doing, so much that she would assign one of her busiest
people to drop everything and come to my farm. I really
think the Blessed Mother loves me. And I am working
night and day for her. I am doing everything I possibly
can. Why not? God is not some kind of employer who
shuns His workers or turns His back on them. God doesn't
play favorites. He rewards His faithful workers! This
contact with His mother could be one of His rewards. It
wouldn't be a gift for only me. It was going to be a gift for
all the people who would end up coming to the farm that
day.

I only had three weeks to get the word out. In a
little over two weeks, close to two thousand five hundred people responded. I almost choked. Where in the
world would we put everyone? How would they even get

on the property? I have major problems with my neighbors and our driveway. I have only a right-of-way and we have been to court over it. What kind of problems was I creating by arranging this?

I had an alternate route off the property, but it was only an old dirt tractor trail through the fields. It was the way all the people came for the first retreat when God stopped the rain, and those that followed, but you can't badger God every time for super big miracles. What if it rained again? I decided that I had to build a new road!

I called a friend, Joe Decker, and he agreed to help. Joe had a great piece of equipment. A four-wheel-drive highlift with a bucket as large as maybe, two yards. Not everything we needed, but pretty good. We also needed a bulldozer and a road grader. The bulldozer I could borrow from my friend, Tom Lower, a local implement dealer. But where would I get a road grader?

I had to speak in Ohio before Maria came. Driving to the talk, I passed what looked like a construction site and sitting there beside the highway was a road grader with a "for sale" sign on it. I love heavy equipment and even owned a backhoe and dump truck at one time. I was always looking at used equipment, but I had never seen a used road grader for sale before. This was quite unusual. Well, it didn't matter anyhow. Who could afford even a used road grader? Curiosity, though, got the best of me that day, because I pulled into the parking lot. I walked over to the office and asked about the grader. There was a man sitting at a desk in an office. A counter divided us and his door was only half-open, so I got his attention by yelling, "How much are you asking for that road grader out there?" He yelled back, "Five hundred dollars." "No, I mean the road grader," I repeated. "Five hundred dollars," he yelled back. He then came out. I asked, "Does it run?" "Of course it runs" he said.

Guess what? I bought myself a road grader for five hundred dollars. We started building the half-mile long road.

It was too costly to build a two-lane road, so we would have to be content with a single lane. Normally there is no traffic at all coming to my farm, so the one lane would only be an issue the day of the event. With so many people coming, I was concerned that we might have a safety problem. If cars are coming in, and an ambulance has to get out, I would need some kind of communication with a person stationed on the main road at the entrance to the driveway to be able to stop traffic. Two-way radios were what I needed. I called a company to come and demonstrate radios. The man brought two kinds: less expensive-one watt radios that he felt they might be of questionable effectiveness in the half-mile distance we needed to bridge, and rather expensive higher wattage radios which he guaranteed would do the job. But there was that high cost.

The man said, "You are very fortunate to live here. Do you see that tower over there?," pointing over the hill. "That is a repeater tower. Even with the cheaper radios, you could hit that tower from here and go 60 miles." He advised me to call the owner and see if we could get on the repeater. I got out my pen and paper and asked him to give me the name and number of the company that owned the tower. He said to call Crown Wrecking. I bought the more expensive radios. I still didn't want to call Crown Wrecking!

The day we started on the road, Joe Decker brought his high lift and I went for the bulldozer. I came back from Tom Lower's with the unit on a trailer. There are big, heavy tracks on a trailer that is used for hauling bulldozers. You fold them down and drive the dozer off. I walked over to one of the tracks and lifted it up. I knew that the weight of the track was about all I could handle because it took all my strength to lift it. What I didn't count on was how difficult it was going to be to lower it down. As I started to lower it to the ground, something snapped in my back and I fell to the dirt. I was paralyzed with pain. It was only with the grace of God that I could get up. I realized instantly what was going on. Satan had just arrived. He did not want this retreat to happen. I said to God, "I know there is a big price to pay for all of the grace that is going to come for everyone. I am willing to pay the price. If it is suffering You want, let me suffer."

This suffering was not going to be the resting-in-bed-and-recuperate type of pain. I was half of the crew available to cut this road in. I worked on the dozer, tractor and grader. Sweat was pouring down my face from the pain. It turned my stomach sour, it hurt so badly. Even that wasn't enough for the enemy. He called for an electrical storm. Neither Joe nor I had never ever experienced such a ferocious storm in our lives. The lightning was striking in the fields all around us. The bolts of electricity hit about every ten seconds and the sound wasn't what you normally hear in thunder. It was like a series of gigantic explosions. The rain was torrential. This was not the kind of weather in which you construct roads. No one in his right mind would sit on steel equipment in an electrical storm, but we were not only doing it, but laughing. We said, "Look at Satan trying to kill us. It's not working."

A car had pulled up on the hill and just parked there. I wondered if the person was a sadist who had come to watch us die. Not hardly! It turned out to be a priest. He was sitting there saying the Rosary for us. Another miracle. What was he doing in a field during a rain storm? This was a private driveway and well off the main road. He just didn't happen by and see us. He was sent.

Pain, rain, exhaustion - we had it all, but we cut the road in three days. We did the impossible. All I needed was the gravel. I called the local limestone mine and asked to have five hundred tons of gravel delivered the next day. The guy on the phone laughed and said, "That would take every truck we have all day long. What do you think, that you are the only customer we have?" "No.

Just do what you can," I said. The next morning I got an early call from the limestone people.

The gravel dealer explained, "It's raining out. Nobody wants gravel when it rains because it costs more. It weighs more when it is wet and you pay by the ton. Do you want gravel today?" "Yes, I do," I said. And I had every truck they had all day long. Normally the delivery trucks would have been unable to drive on what was still a mud road, but as Providence would have it, Mashuda Construction Company donated large amounts of construction fabric to us. It is used as a water barrier so the mud will not push up through the gravel. We rolled that fabric out and the trucks were able to drive over it without getting stuck. At the end of the day, and just the night before the retreat, we had a road. Thanks be to God!

The morning of the retreat there was excitement in the air. Even Bishop Wuerl of the Diocese of Pittsburgh was coming. He had turned down other invitations to our retreats. He was unable to get involved if we had visionaries speaking who were not approved by the Church. When I told him that Maria Esperanza was approved, he requested that I provide him with a signed document with her bishop's seal on it and he would come. I did provide the document and the bishop kept his word. He was coming.

The only bad news for the day was my back. I was still devastated with pain. That morning I had put in an emergency call to a chiropractor and one agreed to see me. After taking some X-rays, he tried to adjust my back. Not a chance. It was as though a thousand knives were stabbing me in my back at one time. I literally had to crawl out of the chiropractor's office to get back in my car. I was still paying the price for Maria's visit.

Maria Esperanza came and delivered quite a message. It was a very powerful day and many conversions happened. After her presentation, I wanted to walk her up to our house so she could get some rest. She'd had problems on her one visit to Canada with people crowding around her, trying to touch her. She had a reputation for being gifted with the power of healing. I had a little army put together to protect her. They surrounded her and walked her down to the podium. The "bodyguards" were all in construction vests (the bright orange ones so that people knew that they were important). I started to feel that they were too intimidating, so I said before leading Maria away, "Stay about fifteen steps back and I will take her by the hand and walk her up to the house and we will get her to safety." I asked everyone in the audience to stay seated and they did.

With Maria's hand in mine, we started walking up the hill to the house. All of a sudden, she bolted from my grasp and by herself, she ran up the highest hill on the farm. She is in her seventies and has a bad heart. She shouldn't have been able to run up that hill. About twenty-five of us finally caught up to her. When she got to the very top of the hill and stopped, she reached down to the ground and picked up a stone. Maria showed me the stone which bore the face of Christ. She then said, "Mr. Rutkoski, one day there will be a church built here." I said, "Mrs. Esperanza, I think the bishop would have a lot to say about that. I work for him. I can't go around building churches. He is the guy who builds churches."

She ignored me. She said, "This is where the altar will be and the church will be in the shape of a cross. The top of the cross will face east. **From the top of the cross there will be a tunnel built to that valley where the Lord told you to build an underground building.**" Maria pointed right at the woods where I had the Stations of the Cross. Sister Louis Marie was one of the twenty-five people in the group around Maria. Every one of them heard her say these things including a newspaper reporter. That is all I needed was to have the press proclaiming that I was going to build a church and an underground building. But Sister was the one who reacted the most. "Oh!" Sister gasped. Maybe she found some confirmation in this. Suddenly I had confirmation from one of the most renowned visionaries alive . . . and one approved by the Catholic Church at that. I started to think about what I was going to do now. Did this mean I would have to start digging a hole in the ground? People are going to think I am nuts!

Maria left and the only thing that hit the papers was her prophecy that a church would be built on my farm. I have since told her, "Maria, building that church is between you and Bishop Wuerl. I am out of that loop. I cannot build a church." But now I was starting to worry about whether, if it were God who asked for this underground building, what if I were offending Him by continuing to put Him off?

I went to my pastor for Confession. "Father, at what point, when God tells you to do something and you don't do it, does it become a sin?" He said, "What are you talking about?" I said, "Well, when God gives you an order, and you ignore it or you give Him too many conditions or challenges to meet, and you don't do it, when does it become a sin?" He said, "What did the Lord tell you to do?" I said, "He told me to build an underground building." Father said to me, "Do you mind if we stand out of the realm of Confession here?" I do not know his reason for this request. Perhaps he did not want to be bound to the contract of silence on this. Father Ken said, "What makes you think God told you to build that building?" My response was that I didn't think it was God, but if it were, I didn't want to tick Him off. That is why I asked God to prove that He was making this request by sending a lot of confirmation.

I detailed the list of confirmations I had received thus far and when I got to the part about Maria Esperanza he said, "Are you *sure* that she pointed to that exact spot and said that you were supposed to. . . ." I interrupted him, "Father, there were twenty-five witnesses there. Do you want to call them all in?" He said, "Well, pray for more confirmation." I said, " That's fine. I will do that, but my question is still, at what point do you stop praying and start doing?" He assured me that I should pray for more confirmation. Okay, Father Ken was the spiritual director for Gospa Missions and I would be obedient to anything he said. Besides, I still didn't have a "yes" on my lips. I just didn't want to offend the Lord after all He had done for me.

Shortly thereafter, all at once, it seemed like everyone who was needed to put a building of this type together was now coming into my life. People started to call me and say, "Mr. Rutkoski, I would like to work for Gospa Missions." I would ask them, "What do you do?" "I'm a builder." Next! "What do you do?" I asked another man. "I'm a cement contractor." The list went on and on. Another man announced that he wanted to work for us. My usual question, "What is it that you do?" He responded, "I am a facilitator." "What's that? I have never even heard of it," I replied. He explained, "I put together construction projects and act as a coordinator. I get all the pieces to pull together." I said, "Oh, my goodness! Welcome aboard."

This group of men, Paul Stalter, Tom Bray and Rich Bartolowits, began to talk among themselves and began to believe in the project. They were anxious to get to work. I was thinking, "Wait a second. I could get in a lot of trouble if people really think that I am going to do this." I was starting to sweat. They wanted to get an architect. I said, "If we get an architect to draw this up, we must not say much of anything to anybody." I was still hesitant about giving a full go-ahead. I wanted to get more confirmation, but it was good to see if all of the pieces fell into place. It could be another way of seeing if this was God.

One of the group said, "I know an architect in Ohio who specializes in this kind of project . . . the waterproofing of underground buildings and everything. I'll call him up." The architect was called and he came out to the farm the very next week.

Lester Zapor is the architect's name. He came and we showed him the project. He said, "Mr. Rutkoski, this project is so big that I couldn't possibly take it on. I'm sorry." I said, "Mr. Zapor, not only do I want you to take this job on, but I want you to do it for free." He kind of laughed and said, "Oh, that changed my mind."

But after a moment he said, "Even if I wanted to do this for free, it is not possible. The doctors tell me I am dying. I am trying to take care of my family affairs now and put things in order before that happens. I'm a very sick man." I said instantly, "Well, I'll make you a deal. I'll pray to God that He makes you well. When He makes you well, you can do the building for free." He laughed and responded, "These guys gave me a copy of the book you wrote. In that book it says that you pray for people and they get well. Is that true?" I said, "What kind of a fool would I be if I went around making deals that couldn't work? You have nothing to lose, do you? If I can't pray for you and have you become well, what's the big deal?"

He said, "Then go ahead and pray for me." I said, "No, not until you agree to the terms. You tell me you will do this building for free, and then I will pray that God makes you well." He answered, "You've got a deal. If God heals me, I will do this building free." I smiled and said, "Not if, pal, *when!*"

I went to church the next morning and after Mass I went in front of the tabernacle and laid prostrate in front of the Lord. I prayed, "There you go, God. If this is You . . . heal the architect! When the architect is well, we can get on with this."

Two weeks later I got a letter from Lester Zapor in which he informed me that all his physical suffering had stopped. He sent the preliminary plans for the building very quickly after that. He worked very hard to squeeze us in. This man put a major architectural project together for something that seemed to be madness to the world.

What does God want with this building? I don't know. To say that my wife was not happy with me constitutes a bit of an understatement. But what do you do when God gives you a mandate? What did Noah go through? Imagine God coming to Noah saying, "Noah, build an ark on this mountain because I am going to cause a flood. You and your family are going to sail away on this ark while everybody else is going to die." I don't know if you have ever heard Bill Cosby's famous comedy routine on Noah

181

and the ark, but at that point, Cosby has Noah saying, "RRRRight!" Me? I'm still saying, " I don't think this is You, Lord." At least I was hoping it wasn't the Lord. I wonder if Noah was like me? Noah went ahead and built the ark. I was still discerning. This was now three years of discernment. The Lord, if it were He, even told me when to have the building completed, but I asked for more time. It seems that the extra time was granted.

I was off one Saturday to shoot the bishop's weekly television show. I volunteer my time to help him when I am not out speaking. One stop I always made on the way was in Pittsburgh so I could attend Mass. Mass was at 7:30 a.m. and I am a stickler for being on time. I would always rush to get there in plenty of time. This particular day I was close to being late. I got off the expressway and came to the stop sign in time to find a caravan of trucks laboring to climb the hill. I was so impatient. This was going to make me late. I was getting very nervous. Please hurry, I was thinking. The last truck approached and, as it passed in front of me so very slowly, I had no problem reading the two-foot letters on the side of the truck that spelled out Crown Wrecking. "Okay, okay, I get it," I murmured. I was starting to cave at that point.

The group of construction advisers that God sent was bent on breaking ground in March or April, 1996. I didn't know what to do. What a heartache. This God stuff can be tough sometimes. I said to them, "Even if we build it, and it is not God's will, we will not let Satan make fools

of us. We'll use this building for good things. We will
use it to store food, medicine, and clothing for Bosnian/
Croatian refugees (from the 1991-1994 war.) It will be of
great help because everything we store in my barn gets
wet. Or perhaps we could raise vegetables on the farm
and supply the local food pantries." That was it! Raise
food for the poor. We will put the building to good use.
Then, if and when God wants it . . . it's His.

I brought the situation to the attention of the board
of directors at Gospa Missions. I laid out the whole scenario and brought the question of this building to a vote.
Father Ken was there and the vote was unanimous.
Build the building. That made me nervous, but the pressure was finally off my head. It felt good to get off the
fence. I was taking almost as long to make my move as
the Church herself would have taken. Hey, maybe I am
finally a true Catholic.

Not so fast. The balloons barely hit the floor. Father
Ken came back to the mission one day and he was really
upset. "I have had it with this Mission. I don't want any
more to do with you and I resign as Gospa Missions' spiritual director." What in the world touched him off? I never
saw him act that way before. And we never gave him one
moment of anything about which to be upset with us. I
said, "Calm down, Father. What is the problem?" "It is
this building," he said. People are coming to me and they
are saying all kind of crazy things and I have had it. I
quit."

"Father, you don't have to quit because of this building. Don't you understand the role of a spiritual director? All you have to do is say that we cannot build this building and it is over. We won't build it. It is that simple. In fact, if you tell me that we can't build it you will make me very happy." Father Ken calmed down. He looked at me and said, "Well, fine, then you cannot build this building." I was overjoyed. "Oh, thank you, thank you, thank you, Father! You have just done me the greatest favor of my whole life. You have taken all of the responsibility of this building off my shoulders and put it on your own. Now God cannot touch me for not doing the building. Obedience is everything. Thank you, Father." I was happier than I'd been in a long time.

Father Ken stopped in his tracks. He said, "Wait a minute. You are not going to do that to me. You build the building!" The building was back on. What a short-lived celebration that was. Father Ken left and we didn't know if we had a spiritual director or not.

It didn't take long to find out. It was announced at Mass one day that Father Ken was leaving the parish and going back to school in Rome for six months and then on to work with the Native Americans in Arizona. I wasn't too sure. I hoped he wasn't running from the responsibility of the building. I wanted to run myself, but to where? You can't hide from God.

The Gospa Missions planning committee said if we were going to build this building we would have to do it by the book. First, we would have to apply for a building permit. A light went on in my head. If this is really God, He could get a permit under any circumstance. We went and applied for the permit to build an agricultural building for agricultural purposes. We also wanted to be able to do some farm research in the building. I was always fascinated with the research program at Slippery Rock College. I did stories on it when I worked in television.

Our request to the local township authorities was turned down. We were advised to file for a zoning change. There was no valid reason for the township commissioners to rule the way they had. It was all farm land and I was already farming it. They said we had to file to make the zoning cover a building for "religious" purposes. That was laughable. It wasn't for religious purposes They would never grant a zoning change for that. Their solicitor must have lied to get out of high school, as I did.

The requirements to have the property rezoned for religion would require fifty-foot roads and I only had a right-of-way, and for only forty feet, at that. But I played their game and went to the zoning board with my (their) request. I kept reminding myself that if all of this were of God, He would make it through. I was called to testify. I started by saying, "You people make me sick. It is little people like you who have caused abortions in this country. You make your little laws and then you make bigger laws and I want nothing to do with you." Obviously I was trying my best not to get a permit.

All of my neighbors had been notified of my request for the variance by the township and several were there. My closest neighbor, a Catholic, was one of those who showed up at the zoning hearing. He tried to see to it that I didn't get a permit. I was surprised by that. We had never had a problem. But he didn't want traffic on his road, even for the two times a year we had our retreats. Gospa Missions is not in the business of offending people. Because of his one objection, we immediately, on our own, moved the retreats off our farm to the Butler Farm Show grounds. The retreats have been there or at the Butler Fair Grounds ever since.

In spite of my best efforts at purposely messing up the situation, in the end, we were given a permit for an agricultural building for agricultural purposes. It was as if this project could not be stopped. They say if something is not of God, it will go away. If it is of God, nothing will stop it. Well, I had one more escape route up my sleeve. I believed if I got out of this in a technical way, God could not hold it against me. But if I just refused, then I had a problem.

Gospa Missions needed a new spiritual director. Where was I going to find a priest who understood me and Gospa Missions enough to help me deal with all of the miraculous events and spiritual difficulties in my life? I thought and thought and came up with nothing. That was my problem. I was thinking rather than praying.

I went down to the church and lay prostrate in front of the tabernacle again. "Please, Jesus, will you help me find a new spiritual director?" As plain as day I heard, *"Father William Kiel."* Do you remember the commercial where the guy hits the palm of his hand on his forehead and says, "I could have had a V8?" That was kind of the way I felt at that point. Why didn't I think of that? Father Kiel and I experienced a miracle together. He would understand.

I asked Father Kiel if he would consider being my and Gospa Missions' spiritual director and his answer was yes. He actually seemed happy about it. I told Father not to be so quick because he was going to inherit a big problem. I explained the building and all of the discernment I had gone through. Father was informed by me that I would be obedient to any decision he made concerning this building. In my mind, I was sure he would never go for it and especially with such an easy way out. Why would he want to be involved with something so controversial? I was home free. Not exactly.

Father Kiel never batted an eye. He actually thought that it was God at work. He had only one question for me. "How does your wife feel about this building?" "She hates the idea. If I even bring it up, she gets very angry." "Fine," Father said. "We will find out if this is God wanting this building. You have to ask your wife's permission to build the building." I cracked up. I said, "Then I have nothing to worry about. She will never agree to build it." "You have to ask," Father said.

I went to my wife and explained what Father Kiel required. "I have to ask your permission to build the building. May I build it?" "Oh, build the building! Build the building! You are going to build it anyhow. Go and build it!" She was not really calm or pleasant about it but I guess it was one woman's way of saying yes.

Father confirmed all of this with Mary and the building was on. The steering committee jumped into action. Bids were solicited and all were more than we could afford to pay, much more than anticipated. I didn't see how it could be done, but at the last minute, Regis, the original contractor who came out to the farm, asked if he could bid on it. He did. The bid was around the amount we raised through the selling of religious goods and we gave the contract to him. The Lord was still showing me confirmation.

A week later I walked out to the back of my farm to have a ground-breaking ceremony. A week after that, there was a huge, gaping hole near the Stations. Excavation was not part of the contract, but Regis said he would find someone reasonable. When I saw that they had to dig through all shale and that it took a week to dig the hole, I shuddered to hear the price. When Rege told me it would cost seventy-five hundred dollars, I could not believe it. That couldn't pay the fuel bill to dig the hole. I asked another contractor what he would have charged to dig the hole and he had quoted fifty thousand dollars. God would not let up on me. It was as though He were saying, "Do you want more confirmation?"

You'd think I would be so embarrassed at what I kept asking the Lord to do, but not me. "Lord, this still seems very crazy. Look at the size of the excavation. It's almost frightening. Could I ask one more thing? Could I see maybe the face of Jesus on a rock?" I took two steps and there was a rock with Jesus on it. I wouldn't even pick it up. As I was running away, I was thinking, "Look at what I put God through." The next day a priest from Nigeria came to visit. I took him back to see the big hole. He said "The ark, the ark." Why would he be saying "the ark?"

I said, "Come here, Father, I want to show you something." Yes, I was taking him over to see the rock. I still didn't believe what I saw. The moment I pointed to the rock, the priest said, "Oh! There is a man on that rock."

"Thomas, Thomas. You certainly are well-named, aren't you?" I said to myself.

A few months later, a priest, Monsignor Miceal Ledwith, a member of the International Theological Commission for the Vatican, caught up to me on a cruise ship. He started asking me about our building.

Do we really want someone from the Vatican knowing about this? About as much as I wanted a hole in my head. I said to him, "What is this to you, Father? Why are you concerned?" I expected to be read the riot act, but instead he announced that he had already built two similar buildings in Ireland. When does it stop?

I could go on and on, but what is the use? Am I a stupid fool for the Lord or what? I now have a big underground building on our farm. The worst that will come of it is some food pantries will get fresh vegetables with which to feed the poor.

All of this is just one guy trying to give a "yes" to God and I am no different from you. At times I slip and I fall. I get angry with my wife and sometimes I yell at her. Then I have to run down to the confessional.

It seems God just deals with average people in an average way. God is not someone who is way off and distant. He is not someone you can't feel or sense. Miracles do happen through Him. He's always there for us. He loves us and all we have to do is return the love. I still don't know what the building is for, but congratulations, Lord, You convinced me.

The entire point of this chapter is discernment. It took over three years to come up with a decision and it entailed much confirmation and spiritual direction. We, as followers of Christ, have to be obedient to the Magisterium and wait for their direction in all Spiritual matters. Many times we hear of messengers and messages calling us to a new or different direction. Do not follow any direction without discerning it over a long period of time and make sure it aligns itself with the Catholic Church. Do not take advice from friends, but call your diocese and ask your questions there. God will respect your desire to discern and move slowly.

Chapter Eleven

Signs in the Sky

Priest sees image

I was invited to be a speaker at a Marian conference at a shrine on Long Island in August of 1996. When we got there, Mary and I carried all of my books and tapes inside. We were instantly shown where to put the boxes. It was a relief to see that the table assigned to us was close to the door because we had to carry the items from our car, which was a long way off. We unpacked and placed the tapes and books on the table for display.

Then we took our seats and the speaker currently at the podium stepped down. The announcement was made that Mass was to begin immediately. The entrance song began. As we sang our hearts out, I could not help noticing that the priest in the procession to the altar was carrying a copy of my book in his hand. I was a little confused. This was the first time this had ever happened.

You would have to know how my mind works to understand what was going on inside my head at that particular moment. "This could be good news or this could be bad news. He must have read the book and enjoyed it and wanted to share his experience with everyone. Good news! Or, if he had read the book and found a problem with it, (although that has never happened) he might want to warn everybody about the book." These were the only two scenarios that came to my mind. What else could it be? The priest had arrived only minutes before he was to say Mass, and besides, I hadn't even had a chance to speak yet! My heart was pounding.

The priest rounded the corner, squared off and faced the congregation. He placed my book on the altar. Now I am more than distracted. I am beside myself with worry. Why is he doing this? What is going on?

The priest welcomed the congregation and introduced himself. He was from Nigeria. (Every time we encounter a priest from Nigeria it brings back a flood of memories of our trip to Ogoja, Nigeria, and of Father Peter Abue. I will tell you about the miracles involving him in the next book) This priest then reached for my book and turned the front cover toward everyone in attendance. He began, "As we drove across Long Island to this conference, a great cloud became visible in the sky. I could not take my eyes off of this cloud. It had the shape of the cross, the shape of the Blessed Mother and more. As we were arriving a bit late, I could not stop to look more closely. We got to the conference center and rushed inside. Entering the door I looked to my right and there was a book laying on a table. This book!" He emphasized the book by raising it higher. "To my amazement, on the cover of this book was the very same cloud that I saw in the sky as we drove here today. I don't know what that means, but I do find it all very amazing."

Father returned the book to the surface of the altar and started Mass. My book, *Apostles of the Last Days,* remained on the altar for the duration of the Mass.

This is not a long, complicated story. It is simply another *Christ-incidence* in a long series of *Christ-incidences* which continually reference themselves to that first book which, it seems, will never cease to amaze me with the events it has brought about.

The image on the cover of that book is a cloud that appeared over my farm on August 5, 1991, in response to a request I made of the Lord. "If this is *really* You, Lord, working in my life, I would like a sign in the sky that I can photograph." I was asking for confirmation because I wanted to give my whole life to Jesus. I believe with all my heart that the sign I requested did appear in the sky as a cloud and the cloud contained the Father, Son, Holy Spirit, the shape of a cross, the Blessed Mother, my face and many other people's faces.

This cloud formation was witnessed by others on the same day, but no one ever made much of it until they saw the pictures I took of it. One man, Ray Ferguson, had his life somewhat altered by his experience with this cloud. Subsequently, he became a volunteer for Gospa Missions and took his faith more seriously.

Ray never told me why he came to Gospa Missions to volunteer. One day his mother called about something and, in the middle of the conversation, she asked me if

Ray ever told me why he came to help. I obviously said no because I didn't know. Ray's mom then told me how Ray had seen the same cloud in the sky on the same day that I did.

This image has followed me around the world as I go evangelizing. People tell me, from time to time, about a very definite cloud shape that appeared over their town before, during or after my visit. I believe it is, in some way, proof that what was being said through me on the night of the presentation was the truth. The message I consistently deliver is: go to Mass every day, say fifteen decades of the rosary each day, fast on bread and water on Wednesdays and Fridays, go to Confession each month, have conversion of the heart every day and lastly, to live in peace. This message will not only change your life, but others around you. It works! Try it.

Image over Montpelier

On Saturday, August 21, 1993, I spoke at Saint Sylvester Church in Graniteville, Vermont. The pastor of the church was Father Francis Eksterowicz. It was a presentation like most others. We prayed the Rosary, celebrated the Holy Mass and I had my opportunity to speak to everyone. After the talk, I prayed over everyone, giving each one there the Blessed Mother's blessing. That talk was the last one of my New England tour, so I went home. I have that standing request of the Lord, which He honors most of the time - if You are going to work a miracle, please wait until I get out of town. I don't want to get blamed for it. This time the Lord honored my request.

A few weeks after I came home, I got a letter from Father Francis. He explained some miraculous events which had occurred the night I spoke at his church and in the following days. I was surprised to hear of those wonderful happenings, but was not informed of the whole story until I sat and talked with Father and Robert Dufresne during a 1997 Gospa Missions retreat in Vermont.

The two filled me in on the rest of the story. The Monday after I had left Vermont, Gail Dufresne, a non-Catholic, rushed off to take her two children to school because they had missed the bus. Robert Dufresne, Gail's husband, a contractor and newly-converted Catholic, was getting ready to go to work. Moments later, Gail came rushing back into the house very excited. "Robert, come quick. I want to show you something," she announced. "What do you want me to see?" Robert asked. Gail continued, "You can't see it from here. Come down to where the driveway meets the road." They both rushed off. At the main road, Gail pointed into the southwestern sky. "Look!" Robert, to his amazement saw a large image in the sky that contained a crucifix. It took up a good portion of the sky.

Robert was surprised by what he saw, but was more surprised by his wife's excitement. Finally there was something they had in common in their faith. Gail asked,

"Doesn't that look like the image that was on that book you brought home Saturday night?" The book was the *Apostles of the Last Days*, which he had purchased at my talk. Robert agreed with Gail, simply saying, "Yes, it does." Still very excited, Gail gave Robert a kiss and grabbed the kids and rushed off for school.

Robert stayed a while looking at the image in the sky, mesmerized. Then he thought to go in to get the book and compare the image on the cover with the one in the sky. He was off to get the book. Returning to the road area, he started to compare the images. He was wondering what this sign from God meant. For whom was it intended, he wondered. He'd had a few little signs before in his newfound conversion and knew they did not happen for no reason at all. Just then, an acquaintance pulled up. It was his subcontractor's wife, Carol Trombly.

Robert hadn't seen her in ages. Carol never came to his house. This day she came to give him some paper work for a job on which he and her husband were working. Robert had a feeling he wanted to show her the cross in the sky, but was a little embarrassed to do so. He hardly knew Carol. He took the paper work from her and said, "Thank you."

Carol was in a hurry, but just before she drove off, Robert got up enough nerve to ask, "Have you ever seen a cross in the sky?" Carol stared at Robert with a puzzled look on her face and said, "No! Why?" Then Robert pointed to the sky. Carol turned and looked up. "Oh, yes, there is a cross there," she said. Robert explains that Carol stopped in her tracks. She looked surprised. She was not rushing off as before. Robert asked Carol, "Does it look this one?" as he showed her my book. With even greater surprise in her voice she said, "Yes, it does." Robert said, "Carol, before you pulled in here I was wondering what all of this meant. That is, when you pulled into the driveway. I have already read this book. I think that this means that you are supposed to have it. Do you want to read it?" Carol said yes and took the book.

A few weeks later, Carol slowly started to relate to Robert what the book was doing for her in her life. Carol had been going through a very stressful time and the book, when she read it, was some sort of answer for her and it touched her deeply. That started a much stronger conversion to God for her. She started making appointments with Father Eksterowicz to be taught on a regular basis about the Catholic faith. She fell in love with God and related to Robert that she was Catholic before, but now she is **Catholic**! Carol now teaches CCD.

The book might have had an impact on Gail's life also, but she never said too much about it. Robert says she has a beautiful faith, but it just isn't Catholic.

Meanwhile, Robert was being bombarded with encouragement from God. He tried to get rid of God and couldn't. He said he got rid of Jesus, but not God. It was God the Father who brought Robert back to Jesus. He said to God, "You can tell me the truth about Jesus. If it isn't true, I can take it." Robert now knows that Jesus died for his sins and Jesus is his Savior. God the Father led Robert to many signs to reveal Jesus to him.

Robert is willing to tell anyone about what he witnessed. Write or call:

> Robert Dufresne,
> 2081 SW Beekman Street
> Port St. Lucie, FL 34953
> Phone 561-343-8751

Illumination confirmation

(The letter which follows adds more to Robert's story:)

Dear Mr. Rutkoski:

I will share my account with you and if you wish to publish it, that's fine! However, even if it only serves to provide you with some encouragement, at least I will not have hidden a light under a bushel basket. The phenomenon I witnessed is not new to you apparently. It has become a common occurrence when you speak. You were standing at the pulpit to the left of the sanctuary, beneath a picture of the Blessed Mother. You were well into your presentation when I noticed some luminosity in the immediate area in which you spoke. There was light surrounding your head and shoulders much as if someone had taken a powerful flashlight and was shining it on the back of your head and upper back. It reminded me somewhat of the many depictions of halos I'd seen in some traditional religious artwork.

The light moved as you did. It followed you. Objects immediately surrounding you seemed to give off a glow. The picture of the Blessed Mother glowed. I am a bit nearsighted and I wore my glasses that evening. I kept removing them to see if the light would still be visible without my glasses. It was. My mind searched for a natural explanation for what I was seeing. Was this some sort of optical illusion? Was it light reflected from somewhere? My wife, Sherla, was present with me and afterwards I asked her if she'd seen any light around you. She stated that she had, but assumed that there was some sort of electric lamp behind you. It was with great relief that I subsequently read the account given by Marie Jenkins in chapter seven of your book, *Apostles of the Last Days*. I was not alone; Marie had also seen "a large, golden glow around the back of your head."

A few days later, I stood with Father Eksterowicz in the spot where you'd spoken and related to him what I'd seen. There was no light fixture of any kind behind you that could account for the phenomenon I'd observed. What does this all mean to me, personally? In my opinion, what I witnessed was a visible confirmation of your mission as a present-day apostle. I believe it was God's way of bestowing His seal of approval. This man speaks the truth! Listen to him.

(Signed)
Mark D. Forgette
P.O. Box 395
East Barre, Vermont, 05649
Phone 802-476-8916

A pastor's testimony

The following testimony is from Father Francis Eksterowicz, then pastor of Saint Sylvester Church in Graniteville, Vermont.

The evening of August 21, 1993, Tom Rutkoski spoke for about one hour at my church, Saint Sylvester in Graniteville, Vermont. If anyone would like to contact me to confirm this testimony, call or write me: Father Francis Eksterowicz, All Saints Church, Richford, VT, 05476, Phone 802-848-7741

Tom came into the church and I instantly noticed that there was a bright light shining on him. He walked forward to speak and the whole church started to fill with light. That bright beam of light followed Tom and stayed with him all during his presentation. I don't go in for this stuff very much, but when it hits you in the head, it hits you in the head. The beam of light that shone on him was very pronounced. Confirmation came through others in the days following his visit. Some in attendance witnessed to me and described the same phenomenon.

Following the presentation, Tom gave a laying on of hands blessing. I myself came up for the blessing. For me it was uneventful, although many others were slain in the Spirit. The following Monday, August 23, 1993, Robert Dufresne called me at 12:00 noon. He related in detail something that appeared in the sky. He said it was the same image that was on the cover of Tom's book. Only because I knew Robert well, did I believe his story. Normally, this is something I would not be interested in. But three corroborative witnesses bolstered the plausibility of the incident: Robert, his wife and Carol (Trombly).

At 2:00 p.m., the final stamp of approval came. God was trying to embed in my mind that this actually happened, and possibly to help me to believe the whole incident of Tom's visit. The confirmation came from Theodore Brennemann,

PhD, a professor of comparative religions at the University of Vermont.

Ted said he was at Tom's talk at Saint Augustine Church in Montpelier and had purchased a copy of his book. He said, "Father you won't believe it, but this morning at around 11:00 a.m., the same image as appears on the cover of Tom's book could be seen here in East Montpelier. The image stayed for approximately 15 to 20 minutes." I assured Dr. Brennemann that I believed his story because I had already had other witnesses call me with similar events. Ted is not an illusionist and his credibility is unquestionable.

For me, it was a sign from heaven - approval for what we heard from Tom and what we all witnessed. This visit has brought confirmation and spiritual benefits to Saint Sylvester Church in Graniteville, Vermont.

[*This concludes the testimony of Father Francis Eksterowicz.*]

I don't know what all we missed from not hearing from all of the twelve original apostles, but I am sure that if these kind of events happen around me, one of the world's bigger sinners, just imagine all that happened to those holy men. It would have been great to have experienced it personally.

Chapter Twelve

The Wrap-Up

I am going to pray for you. This is the same contract I make with everyone. I am going to pray for you every day, three times a day, for the rest of my life. Every morning when I get up, I will kiss the feet of Jesus and I will thank God. I will give Him all my morning offerings and somewhere in there, I'll bring you up. Also, every day at Mass with Jesus Christ alive in me (there is not a more powerful time to pray), I will pray in your behalf. And every night before I go to sleep (for the third time), I will beg in your behalf.

It is a two-way street. I need your help. Pray for me. The orders God gives me are serious ones, at times. They are difficult orders to which to say yes and I need strength. I need great discernment. Pray that God will grant me great discernment. Pray that I will always do His will and that I will never be trapped by Satan. You pray for me and I'll pray for you. Then together, we are going to pray for the priests.

We are going to put this Church back together. We are going to get the plank out of our own eye first, and then we will go help our brothers and sisters get the speck out of theirs. The Protestants have most of the truth; however, we in the Catholic Church, have the whole truth.

If we turned seriously Catholic, the rest of the world would see it, notice it, and come back home. We need the Protestants back home. They out-evangelize us. They are good at what they do. If we made this a one Bread, one Body, community of Jesus Christ again, we could defeat Satan. The way he has us fractionalized into more than twenty-seven thousand different denominations, we are so divided that we will never win this battle.

The Baptists sing so much better than we do. We need them back home, too. Did you ever hear us Catholics sing? Whew! I have heard some good Catholic singing, but for the most part, close the windows so no one hears. But the Baptists get us tapping our feet when we watch a television show and see them in action. I wish we could sing the way those nuns did in *Sister Act*. So we need some Baptists who can teach us how to sing. If only we could get them to come home. Everyone who ever left the Church took a talent with them and we will not be whole until they return.

We have our work cut out for us. We have to take being Catholic in a serious way. A very serious way. God is going to work in all our lives. I will leave you with one story that has opened many hearts already. It happened when I slacked off and I put the Rosary aside for a little while. There is a Scripture that plugs into slacking. *"A little bit of sleep, a little bit of slumber, and poverty will come upon you like a bandit."* Well, I slipped and put the Rosary aside. In three or four days I survived a series of "Christ-incidences" and the Lord spoke to me. He gave me one sentence, *"Thomas, you are neglecting My Mother. If it wasn't for my Mother, I wouldn't be speaking to you now."* How profound!

You can take that statement one of two ways. If the Blessed Mother hadn't interceded on my behalf, what I had been like previous to my conversion could have been so horrible that God was going to give up on me. And maybe it was the Blessed Mother's begging, on my behalf, that changed God's mind. Moses changed God's mind once.

Or you can take it another way. If that little fourteen-year-old girl didn't render her most powerful yes, then none of us would have Jesus Christ as our Savior. He wouldn't be speaking to anyone!

She is the mother of God, our mother! We are not a dysfunctional family. We have a Father in Heaven, a Brother in Heaven and we have a mother in Heaven. That mother has come and asked us, as her children, to go to Mass every day, say fifteen decades of the Rosary every day, fast on bread and water on Wednesdays and Fridays, go to Confession every month and have conversion of the heart every day. Honor your mother. It is a commandment.

The glory of God

Other unusual experiences continue to happen. Once during a presentation I was giving outside, about halfway through, the wind started to blow very hard, and lightning started to flash, only in the area around us. After I was finished talking, everything became peaceful and calm again. A nun came up to me (she had an Irish brogue) and said, "Son, you should have seen it. It was the glory of God behind you." I thought to myself, "Oh, no, even nuns are seeing things!" I was still having a hard time believing these strange stories from people.

Continually, people have reported seeing all kinds of things. I think it is not so much about who or what I am. I believe it is confirmation to people that what is coming out of my mouth is the truth. The truth is what will set us free. I believe it is the glory of our God in action. He intervenes directly or indirectly through the Blessed Mother, saints or just simple sinners like you and me.

These are terrible times. What used to be the safest place on the face of the earth, a mother's womb, is now the most dangerous. Our kids are carrying guns to school. More than fifty percent of marriages are in failure. Can't we read some of the signs of the times? Don't we need miracles? Folks are so quick to say that it's an evil age that seeks signs and wonders. That's true, but is that a reason for the Lord to stop working miracles? That quote doesn't say that the signs and wonders are evil, just the age. It was an evil age when Christ came also. That is precisely why He came. He was working signs and wonders in that evil age to "turn the tide." I believe that is what is going on today. We are so out of control, from the bishops on down to you and me. We are so lukewarm, if not cold or dead, that God is coming with signs and wonders to save us. How many people do you know whom you can honestly say are on fire for the Lord? *"Be hot or cold,"* says the Lord, *"or I will vomit you from my mouth."*

All over the world, people are reporting appearances of the Blessed Mother. Granted, there many more false visionaries than true ones, nevertheless she is on record saying, at one of her apparition sites, that she would appear in every house if she had to. I thank God for a mother like that. I do not have a problem with her wanting to visit every house, as some do. A mother who loves her children would do as much. I can see why she would want to come and be the bearer of these miraculous signs and wonders in these dark days.

It is always her objective to get us to change. She delivers messages so that we might be encouraged to repent. John the Baptist did the same before the coming of Christ. People, as they are, rejected him also, especially the hierarchy of our Church. The truth is that seventy- three percent of all Catholics in America have abandoned their faith because they saw nothing to hold them there. People have more choices now. Creating excitement about our faith is first done in the presentation, and frankly, Jesus isn't being presented in a very exciting way these days in the Catholic Church.

Let me state this statistic one more time: currently, in the United States, only twenty-seven percent of registered Catholics, on average, come to Church on Sunday.

Someone has to help get that number reversed. Some way, somehow, it has to be fixed. If the Catholic Church was a business, it would be bankrupt!

Rather than addressing the gravest of issues at hand, the loss of Catholics, there are those who work hard at stripping our churches of anything that gives them the smallest semblance of holiness and reverence. We bury Jesus in His tabernacle in some back room. We have turned the churches into community social halls which are now called worship spaces. Today, dialogue and personal choices take precedence when Jesus would like to see some good old-fashioned repentance and obedience.

I was away from my Catholic faith for twenty-seven years. In all of those twenty-seven years, not one Catholic ever came for me. Not my pastor, none of the parishioners, and not one word from a Catholic evangelist ever reached my ears. During all those years away from the Catholic Church, do you know who knocked on my door? The Jehovah's Witnesses, the Mormons and the Seventh Day Adventists knocked on it. I saw their television spots and all of their literature.

When do the Sadducees and Pharisees see the writing on the wall? Jesus rose from the dead and is alive. We need to tell everyone that He is still alive in every Catholic Church. This is why you and I have to deal with all of the apparitions and miracles these days. When I was lost and none of you would come for me, Jesus had to do the job Himself! It was a miracle. Our God is now doing most of the work He had asked you and me to do. It seems for the most part that Jesus does the work and does it through miracles. Jesus worked miracles while on earth. He taught all of his disciples to work miracles. He also said:

> *"Amen, amen, I say to you, whoever believes in Me will do the works that I do, and will do greater ones than these, because I am going to the Father.*
> *And whatever you ask in my name, I will do, so that the Father may be glorified in the Son.*
> *If you ask anything of Me in My name, I will do it. If you love Me, you will keep My commandments.*
> *And I will ask the Father, and He will give you another Advocate to be with you always, the Spirit of truth, which the world cannot accept, because it neither sees nor knows it. But you know it, because it remains with you, and will be in you.*
> *I will not leave you orphans, I will come to you. In a little while the world will no longer see Me, but you will see Me, because I live and you will live.*
> *On that day you will realize that I am in My Father and you are in Me and I in you.*
> *Whoever has My commandments and observes them is the one who loves Me. And whoever loves Me will be loved by My Father, and I will love him and reveal Myself to him."* (John 14: 12-21)

God knows what is impeding the process of salvation. He now seems to be showing us all how He can take matters into His own hands. You will never stop God from saving His children.

There was a prophecy to Melanie in La Salette that in the last days, it would be the laity who would evangelize the world. Even Vatican II addressed the laity in a great way. They gave a mandate to our priests. They were told to study the charisms of the laity; encourage the charisms of the laity.

Our Holy Father said, "It's time to kick down the door to the Holy Spirit." You and I, listening to the mandate of our Blessed Mother, must now become "apostles of the last days." You and I need to take on the responsibility of being Catholic and live the message. You will be working miracles in your life soon.

The message of Jesus Christ never changes. It is always constant. What is His message? Change! I need to change my life and you need to change your life.

If we do, other people's lives are going to be changed because of you and me. This is what being a Catholic is all about - getting people to change their lives through the example of having changed.

John the Baptist prepared the way of the Lord by living and shouting repentance from the mountain tops. Simply put, it means change your life. Live for Jesus Christ. Do it His way and you will be a worker of miracles. Do it any other way and you choose a hard and dangerous path to tread.

Jesus said, *"You can tell my followers by these signs..."* So, now do you know what they are?

All of the miracles, excitement, and fun in this book were to get you to this point. This is no less than what Jesus did for the people two thousand years ago. How else would we have gotten you to read all of the words written after each miracle story? How better to convince you to consider living the message?

Plug into your life the Blessed Mother's message of attending daily Mass, praying fifteen decades of the Rosary each day, fasting on bread and water on Wednesdays and Fridays, going to Confession once a month or more and have conversion of the heart every day. Combine these activities with the reading of Scripture, good deeds and lots of love for our fellow human beings. If we hold out to the end, just maybe, we will see each other in Heaven.

I gave you a blessing at the beginning of this journey. Did you figure out what it was? Of course it's the blessing of the Blessed Mother. It is the blessing that was the basis of all of the miracles in this book. She is your mother and wants to lead you to a close personal relationship with her Son, Jesus Christ. That is her job. If you want to love Jesus more, start by loving His mother.

Start by accepting her blessing, living her message and then sharing both withothers.

If you remember, each person who receives her blessing can pass it on. Each person who receives her blessing is aided in his or her conversion. The more it is used, the more powerful it becomes. She says the blessing is like receiving a hug from her. Who would refuse a hug from the mother of Jesus? So now I will give the blessing to you again.

The Blessed Mother's blessing

"I bless you with the blessing of the Blessed Mother and may the power of the Holy Spirit come upon you."

In Luke's Gospel, Jesus relates:
"That servant who knew his master's will but did not make preparations nor act in accord with his will shall be beaten severely; and the servant who was ignorant of his master's will but acted in a way deserving of a severe beating shall be beaten only lightly. Much will be required of the person entrusted with much, and still more will be demanded of the person entrusted with more. I have come to set the earth on fire, and how I wish it were already blazing!" (Luke 12: 47-49)

This book may very well be your second chance. I pray that it has set you ablaze. Now, as a very blessed person, go out and work miracles. The sheep of this flock have been scattered. The shepherds need our prayers.

The world is waiting to witness the truth and it must come from you. You are to be an apostle of the last days.

Thomas Rutkoski

Epilogue

On the day I was sending my first book, *Apostles of the Last Days,* to the printer, I received a fax that made me realize the significance of the title. Then moments before completion, I placed that explanation in the book under the heading "Epilogue." It is truly ironic, 'a Christ-incidence,' that the same scenario happened again. The cover of this book depicts me as a child, sitting in a chair, and in the confines of this book, it is mentioned how we have to become as children. The day I was rushing to get this book to the printer the gospel at Mass was as follows:

At that time, the disciples came to Jesus and asked, "Who is the greatest in the kingdom of heaven?" He called a child, whom he put among them, and said, "Truly I tell you, unless you change and become like children, you will never enter the kingdom of heaven. Whoever becomes humble like this child is the greatest in the kingdom of heaven. Whoever welcomes one such child in my name welcomes Me. If any of you put a stumbling block before one of these little ones who believe in me, it would be better for you if a great millstone were fastened around your neck and you were drowned in the depth of the sea. Woe to the world because of stumbling blocks! Occasions for stumbling are bound to come, but woe to the one by whom the stumbling block comes!" (Matthew 18: 1 - 7)

An Invitation

As a disciple of Jesus, your responsibility is great, so I invite you to accept the challenge of doing much more for God. Your first priority should be the honest support of your parish and diocese. With so few attending Mass, the collections are down in many places and there are fewer people to volunteer their time.

After fulfilling your commitment to the Church, I invite you to become part of Gospa Missions (Our Lady's Missions) and be an Apostle of the Last Days. You can do this in several ways. If you have the ability to lay your current life aside, if you are healthy and financially solvent, think about coming to Gospa Missions to work with us. We need a few good professionals to work at the Mission headquarters. Local volunteers are always welcome to help out a few hours or a few days a week at our religious store or in the office. Contact us to see if your talents will fit into our needs.

Shopping for all of your religious goods at our *Amazing Grace* store in Evans City, PA, on the internet at gospa.org or catholicbookstore.org or through our Gospa Missions mail order department will have you involved in God's work. How? Because we are non-profit and all proceeds support the Mission and our humanitarian activities. God asks for 10% of our time, talent and treasure. I am only suggesting ways to do just that.

It is people like you who set up all of the places where I speak. You could invite me to your conference, set up one presentation or a whole tour in your area. Contact me for a speaker portfolio. At each presentation we can do a healing service, if you desire. So all you have to do is pick a subject, call me to set the date, and find a place to do it. I can give up to five different talks which can be your parish mission or Life in the Spirit seminar. I could give a presentation at your grade school, high school or CCD program. I love speaking to kids. The talks I have delivered to prison inmates have been very special to me, as well. I do not charge a stipend and the airfare is not even always required, so it could cost you nothing.

You could support this Mission through the Gospa Missions newsletter. It is one of the best periodicals in the business. The short and simple teachings, devotions, prayers, information on the saints, book and video reviews and hard-hitting editorials will help you to stay rooted in your faith. Consider subscribing.

Financial assistance for our orphanage in Ogoja, Nigeria, Africa, or sponsorship of a child would be great.

I ask people who want to support my evangelizing or see that the book gets into the hands of people who cannot afford it, to send a $20 donation. I ask $20 from all of you who read the book (even if it was just loaned to you or if you already paid for it,) if it helped you in your spiritual journey. It will help us help others.

Donations have come. From $20 to a high of $7000 at one time, came in envelopes, as people voiced their support for Catholic evangelists and expressed their desire to help spread the Good News. They added their prayers and they made Gospa Missions grow to be a powerful force against Satan. With their help, we distributed 25,000 free copies of *Apostles of the Last Days*. We have sent books, tapes, and videos to prisons, the military and to the less fortunate all over the world. You can continue this tradition by sending a donation yourself. Send what you can and we will maximize your gift. This means that your donation will not go to furnish some executive with a big salary. The highest paid person at Gospa Missions receives only seven thousand dollars a year. I, myself, did not received a paycheck for more than eight years. I will be prudent with your donation.

If you would like to write me, my address is:

Thomas Rutkoski
333 Wilderness Trail
Evans City, PA 16033

Whatever you decide to do, may God bless you.

In the love of Christ,

Thomas Rutkoski
Founder, Gospa Missions

Other works by Thomas Rutkoski

Books
Apostles of the Last Days
Coming soon - order now! Tom's new book-
I Want to be a Saint

Video Tapes
Conversion Story
The Responsibility of Being Catholic

Audio tapes
Conversion Story
The Responsibility of Being Catholic
Miracles in My Life
Tom Talks to Kids (7-14)
Tom Talks to Teens (15-20)
God's Winning Team
In Giving, You Receive

Popular Products from Gospa Missions

Crucifix-medal of St Benedict
Our Lady of Grace (The Tihaljina statue)
Image of Jesus Prints
The Pope with the Blessed Mother Prints

Above products available through Gospa Missions by mail or
on the web at **www.gospa.org** or
www.catholicbookstore.org